WHY POSITIVE SELF-TALK WORKS!

As much as 77% of what you tell yourself may be working *against* you! In this life-changing book, you'll discover how the simple, revolutionary technique of Self-Talk can reverse negative programming, and fill your life with new, vital energy.

1) External solutions are temporary. The Self-Talk program leads to *permanent behavioral change,* because *you* control all the messages—silent, spoken, or written—that your brain receives.

2) Self-Talk is based on the latest scientific developments about how the human brain receives and accepts information. If you want to make a change and make it stick, you've got to do it the way the brain works.

3) This *new, word-for-word* programming changes the conditioning of the subconscious mind—the control center of the brain. This specific vocabulary can be used by anyone, at any time, to replace negative programming with positive, new, *repeated* directions.

TALK TO YOURSELF!
LEARN THE WORDS—THE *RIGHT* WORDS—
AND USE THEM!
MAKE SUCCESS A PERMANENT WAY
OF LIFE, WITH . . .
WHAT TO SAY WHEN YOU TALK
TO YOUR SELF!

Books by Shad Helmstetter

Choices
Finding the Fountain of Youth Inside Yourself
Predictive Parenting: What to Say When You Talk to
     Your Kids
The Self-Talk Solution
What to Say When You Talk to Yourself
You Can Excel in Times of Change

Published by POCKET BOOKS

For information regarding special discounts for bulk purchases,
please contact Simon & Schuster Special Sales at
1-800-456-6798 or business@simonandschuster.com

WHAT TO SAY WHEN YOU TALK TO YOUR SELF

Shad Helmstetter, Ph.D.

POCKET BOOKS

New York   London   Toronto   Sydney

POCKET BOOKS, a division of Simon & Schuster, Inc.
1230 Avenue of the Americas, New York, NY 10020

Copyright © 1982 by Shad Helmstetter

Published by arrangement with Grindle Press

All rights reserved, including the right to reproduce
this book or portions thereof in any form whatsoever.
For information address Grindle Press, c/o Avalon Corporation,
8340 East Raintree Drive, Suite B-2, Scottsdale, AZ 85260

ISBN 13 : 978-0-671-70882-5
ISBN 10 : 0-671-70882-1

First Pocket Books printing April 1987

35 34 33 32 31 30 29 28

POCKET and colophon are registered trademarks of
Simon & Schuster, Inc.

Printed in the U.S.A.

This book is dedicated, with love, to my parents, Fred and Nora Helmstetter—to my mother, who taught me persistence and perseverance, and to my father, who taught me that there is always a better solution.

ACKNOWLEDGMENTS

Among the many fine individuals who have helped make this book possible, I would like to express my gratitude to the patience of my wife, Dellayne, to my friend and associate William Wallace, whose belief and support have been without peer, and to my son Anthony, who lived the principles of this book before it was written. I would also like to thank Julia Hayes who was willing to be a dedicated partner and pioneer in the new frontier of human potential, to my senior editor, Ré Ann Brown, whose contributions to the content and concept of this book were invaluable, and to my copy editor Holly Hill, one of the finest word-smiths I shall ever hope to meet. I owe a special debt of gratitude to Sylvia Regelbrugge who, for some forty years of my life, has unfailingly encouraged and always believed. I would like to offer a special thank you to my teacher and friend, Barbara Baylis, who taught me, many years ago, who I am. I would also like to extend my warmest thank you to my friend Ray Lindstrom who possesses both genius and belief, to Gregory, who has inspired me more than he knows, to Jeffery, who is becoming a true achiever, and to Timothy, my youngest son, who would have felt terribly left out if I did not mention him by name.

CONTENTS

CONTENTS

WHAT TO SAY WHEN YOU TALK TO YOUR SELF

CHAPTER ONE

Looking for a Better Way

You are everything that is,
your thoughts, your life, your dreams come true.
You are everything you choose to be.
You are as unlimited as the endless universe.

LIFE, FOR MOST of us, should be pretty good.

We have all heard what life is *supposed* to offer: endless opportunities, the fulfillment of our dreams, and a chance to live each day in a way that brings happiness and success. Most of us want and need at least a successful job or career, a good family life, and reasonable financial security. We expect that from life. We know deep inside that we deserve our fair share and we have every right to attain it.

Have you ever wondered, then, why things don't work out the way they should? Why do we not get from life many of the things we would like to have— and know we should? Why do some people seem to be "lucky," while the great majority of the rest of us seem not to be?

Why are some people, day to day, happier, more productive, more fulfilled than others? What makes the difference? Is it Kismet, a kind of fate, which in some mysterious way charts our destiny and leaves little of the steering of our course through life up to us?

Is the control of our lives in our hands or isn't it? And if we can, or *should* control our lives, what goes wrong? What holds us back? If we truly would like to do better, be the way we really would like to be, and be happier and more successful every day in every area of living, *what is the wall that stands in our way?*

AN UNLIMITED LIFE OF PRACTICAL POTENTIAL

Imagine living a life which did not give in to the barriers and the battlements, the hassles and the hurdles of everyday living. Imagine a life filled with the vitality of achievement and the enrichment of daily self-fulfillment. To me, for a long time, that kind of life sounded like an impractical dream, a cardboard box filled up with daydreams and wishes. To live a life of hope, promise, expectation, and achievement was to live the life of someone who lived only in the pages of a book.

When I was quite young I had a soaring imagination. Long before I learned what we could *not* do, I dreamed of doing what I knew we *could*. I remember, as a young boy, lying on my back in the cool, wet grass late at night, my mind sinking into the depths of the crystal clear stars that blanketed the summer sky above me. I could reach out and touch those stars. I could imagine any dream and see it come true.

It was only later that my dreams gave way to more practical considerations. Star-filled heavens, dew-soaked grass, and princely dreams of imaginary kingdoms bowed to more rational requirements. As I began to pursue my education in earnest, I began to learn what we could *not* do. In time I became more intent on studying the laws and the limits of man, than on learning the far-reaching extremities of mankind's potential.

I learned all of the "shoulds," "musts," and "can-*nots*." I was told that it was bad to have your head in the clouds and it was good to have your feet on the ground. So I extracted my head from the magical excitement of the universe and got down to business learning about the more practical matters of survival and acceptance. From time to time I had the nagging suspicion that there was more to all of this than was meeting the eye—I just couldn't see it yet.

It was years before I decided it was time to stop and look at the stars again. But I did. The result of that one small decision changed my direction and my life.

By the time I stopped and sank once again, up-wards, into the stars, I had completed a twenty-year odyssey which took me from the backroads of a farmland village to the towering offices of New York's Madison Avenue; from a quiet countryside of wheat fields to the negotiating tables of three-piece-suited attorneys and well-groomed marketers. My odyssey took me to snow-covered midwestern college campuses, and to palm lined streets of western universities.

Somewhere, during that time, I began to wonder and

dream again, as I had as a young boy years before. What if we *could?* I wondered. What if we could find what's stopping us and turn it around? What if there *is* an answer and no one else has looked in the right place? What if any of us, at any time, could reach up *and touch the stars?*

I began the first part of my search by studying something called "human behavior." That's something you can get a degree in without ever really figuring it out. It is also something that older people seem to know more about than younger people. No matter how many educational degrees my professors could profess, I suspected that some of the grayed and silver-haired older people I knew had figured out what human behavior was all about long before we were taught courses in the subject.

I next studied something called motivational marketing. That teaches us what makes people do what they do even when they don't want to do it. When I completed my course work, it was my final opinion that you can never really get anyone to do anything they don't want to do unless you use force. I decided that in most of the free world, "force" is called advertising.

In time I found myself walking the hallways of academic psychology. It is a good field and it deserves our attention and respect. A lot of people have lived richer lives because someone who cared took the time to listen.

Eventually I embarked upon a journey of my own. Nowhere in my studies of mathematics, business, religion, or psychology, had I found a concrete solution to the question of how the average individual could touch all the stars in his or her heaven and still keep both feet on solid ground. I knew there had to be a better way, something that was obvious perhaps, something that might have been overlooked. I believed that mastering one's future must surely start with managing one's "self." And if we could accomplish that, we could manage and master at least a part of what we call "life."

As I continued to study the inner workings of the human mind, I began to look for the answers—the "solutions" which others most certainly must already have found. I found dozens of answers. But I discovered only one solution.

CHAPTER TWO

The "Answers"

THERE IS ALWAYS an answer, of course. There are countless self-help "answers," which any of us can find in any bookstore. If we are to believe what we read on the dust jackets of self-help best-sellers, all any of us has to do is read the right book and, beginning tomorrow, we will be able to change what we would like to change, live better, and find the achievement each of us is seeking.

Having spent more than twenty years studying most of the literature of "success," I have found a consistent, unfulfilled promise—the promise of our success, waiting just around the corner.

I have learned that I can be hypnotized, processed, or reborn (and not just in the religious sense). I know that I can attend seminars which will give me the "answer." I can become a goal-setter and a "true achiever." I can learn to organize my day, set my priorities, and accomplish more than I ever dreamed possible. I can learn to "think positively," be more creative, relate to others and become "centered." I have learned that success is mine for the taking; all I have to do is accept my destiny of achievement and greatness. I have read great words of wisdom and been told that I can change anything in my life I choose to change.

And yet, after learning these great and marvelous truths, and some of them are, I would take with a grain of salt anyone's claim that they can give you the "secret of success." If anyone offers you the moon, don't buy it.

As much as I have been a student of success, I have also been a skeptic. For many years I read and studied and listened. And I wondered: If there are so many "keys" to success, why aren't they working? Why are there shelves full of self-help best-sellers? It seemed to me that if the books were working as they ought to work, we wouldn't keep needing new ones. If there are so many answers to our questions about what to do to make life better, why have so many people failed at making these great ideas work? Or if they work for a time, what makes them stop working?

Have you ever attended a "pep rally" or a meeting in which someone gave a rousing motivational speech? Why didn't it last? Have you ever been inspired to change, to achieve, and then stopped? Where did the inspiration go?

The problem is not with the books. The problem is not with the seminars or with the motivational talks. There are a lot of self-help ideas and techniques that are good. They *should* work—and they *could*. But they don't work, or they don't keep working, because of something that all of us overlooked: *That's not how the brain works*.

The human brain, that incredibly powerful personal computer control center that each of us has, is capable of doing for you anything reasonable that you'd like it

19

to do. But you have to know how to treat it. If you treat it just right, and carefully give it the right directions, it will do the right thing—it will work for you in the right way. But if you give your mental computer the wrong directions it will act on those wrong directions; it will continue to respond to the negative programming that you and the rest of the world have been giving it without even being aware of it.

THE 148,000 "NO'S!"

I'll give you an example of some of the negative programming most of us have received. During the first eighteen years of our lives, if we grew up in fairly average, reasonably positive homes, we were told "No!," or what we could *not* do, more than *148,000 times!* If you were a little more fortunate, you may have been told "No!" only 100,000 times, or 50,000 times—however many, it was considerably more negative programming than any of us needs.

Meanwhile, during the same period, the first eighteen years of your life, how often do you suppose you were told what you *can do* or what you *can* accomplish in life? A few thousand times? A few hundred? During my speaking engagements to groups across the country, I have had people tell me they could not remember being told what they *could* accomplish in life more than three or four times! Whatever the number, for most of us the "yes's" we received simply didn't balance out the "no's." The occasional words of "belief" were just that—occasional—and they were far outweighed by our daily doses of "cannots."

This negative programming that we all received (and still receive) has come to us quite unintentionally. It has come to us from our parents (who wanted to protect us); it has come to us from our brothers and sisters, from our teachers, our schoolmates, our associates at work, our lifemates, advertising of all kinds, the morning paper and the six o'clock news.

Leading behavioral researchers have told us that as much as *seventy-seven percent* of everything we think is negative, counterproductive, and works against us. At the same time, medical researchers have said that as much as seventy-five percent of all illnesses are self-induced. It's no wonder. What if the researchers are correct? That means that as much as seventy-five percent or more of our programming is the wrong kind. Until very recently no one understood well enough the human mind—how it really works. The result was that without knowing what they were doing, and with us not recognizing the immense effect this "casual" programming was having on us, "they" have been programming us in the wrong way. Everything and everyone around us, without being aware of it, has been programming us.

Unfortunately, most of it was the wrong kind of programming—and we took it to heart. Year after year, word by word, our life scripts were etched. Layer by layer, nearly indelibly, our self-images were created. In time, we ourselves joined in. We began to believe that what we were being told by others—and what we were telling ourselves—was true. No matter how innocently given or subtly implied, we began hearing the same words and thoughts repeatedly; hundreds, even thousands of times we were told, or we told ourselves, what we could not do, could not accomplish. *Repetition is a convincing argument.* Eventually we believed what others told us and what we told ourselves most; we began to live out the picture of ourselves we had created in our minds.

In time we became what we most believed about ourselves. And in so doing, we created a wall, which for most of us will stand invisibly but powerfully between us and our unlimited futures for as long as our old programming remains in force. Unless the programming we received is erased or replaced with different programming, it will stay with us permanently and affect and direct everything we do for the rest of our lives.

Fortunately, that doesn't have to be the case.

THE END RESULT
OF YOUR OWN THOUGHTS

I was quite young when I first heard the Biblical passage which reads, "As a man thinketh, so is he." I recall shaking my head, thinking that could not be. How could we possibly *be* what we think? After all, isn't our physical self one thing and our private thought another? Little did I (or most of us then) understand that the Biblical passage had hit the nail of truth squarely on the head. It would be years later, however, after much research, and following the discoveries through which modern-day neuroscientists had begun to unlock the secrets of the human mind, that I would come to know just how correct—how *scientifically* correct—that Biblical passage had been.

In the last two decades we have learned more about

the workings of the human brain than was known throughout all history prior to that time. We now know that by an incredibly complex physiological mechanism, a joint effort of body, brain and "mind," we become the living result of our own thoughts. Through scientific discovery we have proved the relationship between our own "mental programming" and the matter of whether we will succeed or fail in any endeavor we undertake in life, from something as important as a lifetime goal to something as small as what we do in a single day.

Have you ever considered just how much of what you do—how you act, how successful you are—is dependent on the conditioning, the programming you received from others and on the conditioning you subsequently bought and kept giving yourself? It is virtually impossible for any of us to do anything, no matter how insignificant, without being affected by our conditioning. Every step you take, move you make, or word you say is affected.

It follows that if every action you take, of any kind, is affected by prior programming, then the end results of your actions are equally affected—in short, how successful you will be at *anything* is inexorably tied to the words and beliefs about yourself that you have stored in your subconscious mind. And what is stored there, for most of us, was decided for us by someone else.

Think for a moment what you might do differently tomorrow if you were someone else—someone whose programming was different from yours. Or what might you do differently if you had been brought up with a completely different, more positive set of attitudes and beliefs and feelings from those which you may have now—attitudes and beliefs and feelings which in every case would assure you of having an abundance of self-belief, enthusiasm, and achievement?

WHAT COULD YOUR FUTURE HOLD?

If you had just the right kind of successful new mental program, would you be doing the same thing for a living that you are doing now? Would you be doing your job in exactly the same way? What about your personal life? Would you change anything, improve anything? Would you have reached any more goals than you have reached? Would you have more money in the bank or any more financial security than you have now? What about your day-to-day life— would it be less frustrating and more rewarding? And, with different preparation or conditioning, what could your future hold? Would it be the same as your future holds for you today, or would it be better?

What if each and every day, from the time you were a small child, you had been given an extra helping of self-confidence, double the amount of determination, and twice the amount of belief in the outcome? Can you imagine what tasks you might accomplish more easily, what problems you would overcome, or what goals you could reach? After all, success, ultimately, is up to the individual. It isn't the pen—it's the writer; it isn't the road—it's the runner that counts.

Why is it, then, that some accomplish nearly any task more easily than others, achieve their goals more readily, and live their lives more fully? Could it be that those who appear to be "luckier" than the rest have actually only gotten a little better programming, or perhaps have learned how to erase their old negative programming and replace it with something better?

After examining the philosophies, the theories, and the practiced methods of influencing human behavior, I was shocked to learn the simplicity of that one small fact: You will become what you think about most; *your success or failure in anything, large or small, will depend on your programming—what you accept from others, and what you say when you talk to yourself.*

It is no longer a success theory; it is a simple, but powerful, fact. Neither luck nor desire has the slightest thing to do with it. It makes no difference whether we *believe* it or not. *The brain simply believes what you tell it most.* And what you tell it *about you*, it *will* create. It has no choice.

At the time I first recognized that this one simple clue could lead to a breakthrough in individual attitude and performance, most of what we thought we understood about the human brain was little more than speculation. Medical researchers and mind/brain scientists had not yet explored or mapped the mazes of the brain to the extent to which they have today. Few of the brain's complex electro-chemical mysteries were fully understood. Even today the brain is only just beginning to give up its secrets. Each day more progress is made and researchers have learned to anticipate an unending drama of new discoveries.

There was good reason for my excitement over my own rediscovery of the ancient truth which told us that "what we think is what we become." There were tens of thousands of devout believers who, through one religion or another, were professing the same "truth." To them it was inevitable, I suppose, that scientific research would one day prove their claim: that we control with our own minds most everything in our lives, including our health, our careers, our personal relationships, and our futures.

But to me it was the scientific understanding of *how* the process *worked* which so ignited my interest. What if, I wondered, we could begin to understand the workings of the mind so thoroughly that we could actually learn how to change or override our old programming and replace it with a specific, word-for-word new program? And what if we could do it in such a way that we could affect and improve our attitudes and our behavior fast!—not through years of difficult study or training, but easily and simply, anytime we chose to!

That is exactly what the brain will do. An understanding of that simple function of our own personal computer—the human brain—is what has been missing from most of the books and most of our motivational talks. An understanding of that one simple requirement of our mental machinery can help us make a simple but vital change in how we accept programming from others—and, more importantly, what we say when we talk to ourselves.

CHAPTER THREE

What Works and What Doesn't

THE DISCOVERY OF any new thing of value is a time of excitement. And like the dreams we had as children, of finding chests of gold doubloons and priceless jewels, there is a part of us that keeps seeking the treasure. But instead of looking for rubies and gold, I found myself searching for a single small key—one that would unlock a door I knew must lead to a better life for many.

I was searching for something that I sensed had been missing from the books and messages and solutions of so many who had come before me. It became obvious to me that if the final solutions to a better life, more happiness, and personal fulfillment had already been discovered, then *something vital was missing;* something that was so essential, so important to the whole process of achieving success, that without it, the other solutions would not work, at least not for any length of time.

I began to recognize that this "missing ingredient" could be the glue which would, for the first time, bind

27

all the other elements of success and self-fulfillment together.

One look around told me that my first assumptions were correct: even the best-selling success "solutions" were able to create *lasting* changes in only a handful of the tens of thousands of people who tried them. They would work for a time and then the average individual would revert to his old ways. After the first excitement of the brand new self-belief wears off, the dreams soon give way to the realities of everyday living.

Since the old programming controls the habits, it is the old habits which once again take over. The new goal of conquering the world and making great changes (which sounded so good in the book) is left to be tackled again some other day. I would prefer to be more optimistic, but how many people do you know who really have their lives totally "together," (which means something like being "successfully successful") day after day, year after year? It has been proved that it is not impossible to live a full and rewarding life, day in and day out—it's just highly unusual.

So even though we were told that any of us could live highly successful lives, and we were given specific instructions as to how to go about it, very few of us actually have done it. At least not for longer than a few weeks or a few months. Then it's back to the "old" way, just like before, living life as we always have, maybe getting a little ahead or getting by, and wondering why we aren't doing as well as we think we should.

Even the very best ideas which we found in best-selling books, even the ones that looked like they would work for certain, would work for a while and then slowly lose their importance in our lives. Exciting ideas, great breakthroughs and inspirations for the mind which seemed to offer so much, became once-read books sitting forgotten on a shelf.

Could it be, I wondered, that the missing ingredient I sought was somehow connected to our individual programming? In order to learn that answer, and in order to learn what *does* work, I decided that it would help to first understand what does *not* work—and *why*.

ON THE TRAIL
OF A SENSIBLE SOLUTION

Of all the self-help concepts I have uncovered, the concept of "programming" the brain with a more successful "new picture" of yourself is the most sensible. I am not the first behavioral researcher or author to figure this out. Others have come to the same conclusions as I, that whatever you put into your mind—*in one way or another*—is what you will get back out—*in one way or another*.

Although not every writer in the self-development field has arrived at the same conclusions (only because they were looking at the problem in a different way), there are those who have written books and shown millions the way to a better life—if not permanently, at least for a time. And while they were leading others toward happiness and a more abundant life, I was busy watching the great philosophies of success. In time I began to analyze why only a few of the success principles worked and why most did not.

I studied the philosophies of success, analyzed the lists of instructions—the "how-to's" of making more money, being better managers, losing weight, overcoming depression, getting a better job, setting goals, living with others, managing time, or just generally "being more successful." I tried the success techniques for myself and talked to dozens of others from many walks of life who had done the same. I talked at length with many of the leaders of the success industry—corporations whose business it is to sell us success.

I talked to the customers who attended the seminars, bought the books, or listened to the cassettes. I talked to the employees of the companies who were in the business of selling success formulas, to learn if they, too, applied the principles which their companies promoted. To learn what really "worked," and what did not, I immersed myself in the world of success, examining every facet of that fascinating field from the inside out. I consulted with the leaders of the industry. I examined their methods, their systems, and their "solutions."

During those years of observing, practicing the techniques, and analyzing the results of others, I continued to ask myself the question: If there are so many *good* solutions, why aren't they creating *permanent* changes in our lives? As an example, why do so many people who read a book on something as worthwhile as "positive thinking" decide to start thinking differently and end up, six months later, thinking just as they did before they read the book? Eventually I came to some clear conclusions about "self-improvement":

1) Most of the authors are on the right track. For the most part, they appear to be sincere, caring individuals—true believers in the very best for the human race.

2) If you follow their advice, most of it will help.

3) If you stop following their advice, invariably it will stop working. Some of the "success principles" I studied work longer (without continued effort) than others. However, nothing you read once is permanent; none of the self-help programs continue to work by themselves or without *constant* reinforcement.

THIRTY YEARS OF "HOW-TO'S"

You may or may not be aware of the kinds of "self-help" concepts I am talking about. In case you haven't spent a lot of time improving yourself through the reading of self-help literature during the last twenty or thirty years, I will summarize its most popular teachings for you. The literature says that if you want to be more successful, you should:

Believe In Yourself
Keep Your Priorities Straight
Take Responsibility For Yourself
Create Your Own Future
Focus On What You Want
Learn To Visualize The Outcome Of Your Goals
Never Let Anyone Control Your Destiny For You
Be Creative
Think Big
Control Stress
Be Aggressive And Assertive
Think Positively

WHAT TO SAY WHEN YOU TALK TO YOUR SELF

Chart Your Own Course
Set Specific Goals And Review Them Often
Spend Some Time Each Day Improving Your Mind
Review Your Results And Readjust As Necessary
Be Tolerant
Do Everything With Love
Don't Hate
Have Courage
Recognize That Most Of What We Believe About Life
Is An Illusion
Be Honest
Work Hard
Believe Money Is Good And
It Will Come To You
Have Faith
If You Agree To Do It, Enjoy It
Be Strong
Show Affection
Manage Your Time
Dress Right
Learn To Sell Yourself
Take Time Off
Believe In A "Higher Self"
Eat Right
Live Prudently
Seek The Aid Of Others Who Are In Sympathy
With Your Goals
Give Assistance To Others
Keep Motivated
Meditate
Be Optimistic
Trust Others And Be Worthy Of Trust
Recognize That Success Is More Than Money
Be Kind
See The "Big Picture"

WHAT TO SAY WHEN YOU TALK TO YOUR SELF

Take Care Of The Details
Get Organized
Don't Procrastinate
Stay In Control
Keep Fit
See Problems As "Opportunities"
Learn Everything You Can About Your Job
Don't Be Afraid Of Success
Be Generous To Others
Believe In God
Reach A Little Higher Than You Thought You Could
Set Your Sights
Take Action
Never Give Up

If you do all that, I have been told, you will be successful.

Even being skeptical, I had to agree. If you combined the best of all the self-help or self-improvement teachings available to us, it is clear they have given us most of the "keys to success."

If that is true—and I believe that it is—then what's wrong? If the principles, and in many cases even the detailed instructions, are all clearly outlined for us, why do we need more books, more solutions, and more reminders?

In a recent year it was estimated that more than $200 million worth of self-help books and materials were purchased in the U.S. alone! That's quite an industry. With all of that, what is missing? What is the missing key? What would complete the puzzle and offer each of us lasting, individual success and fulfillment?

THE MISSING INGREDIENTS

In my analysis of what worked and what did not, I found three ingredients which are clearly missing from almost *all* of the literature:

1) The first missing ingredient is *permanence*. All "external" solutions are *temporary*. Even the best of the ideas work only for a time. Without constant attention and effort, even the most exciting success breakthroughs run their course and eventually end up on our list of "good ideas" and "good intentions." Few, if any, offered built-in ways to keep them working. I have yet to find a book that would jump down off the shelf and tap you on the shoulder each morning and say, "Hey! Remember me? Remember what I taught you? Why aren't you still doing it?"

2) The second ingredient missing from most of the success literature is *a knowledge of the physiological processes of the human brain—based on what we now know about actual mind/brain functions*. Without an understanding of the actual process by which the human brain accepts information (programming) and, in turn, responds, directs and controls us, it would be difficult (or impossible) to create any success plan that worked and kept working indefinitely.

The brain runs the ship. If you want to make a permanent change of any kind, you've got to follow the rules. If you want to make a change and make it stick, you've got to do it the way the brain works.

3) The third missing ingredient, and the most important of all, is *a new, word-for-word set of directions, new programming to the subconscious mind (the control center of the brain)*. That means a specific "programming vocabulary" which is worded in a specific way, that anyone can use at any time, to erase and replace the old negative programming with positive, productive new directions.

The only solution which includes all of the three missing ingredients is something called Self-Talk.

Think for a moment about some of the things you would like to accomplish or achieve in your life—or even those smaller things you would like to change about your life right now. Your objective could be to earn more income, have a better family life, improve your skills, do better in school, do better at work—anything at all.

Whatever means you choose to make the change, unless you first begin to change your old "programming," the years of conditioning that keeps you doing it the *old* way, the likely outcome is that what you want to accomplish will not work—or will not last.

CHAPTER FOUR

New Discoveries

DURING THE LAST few years, neuroscientists have learned that much of what we had suspected about the human brain is true: The brain operates very much like a personal computer. It's not that simple, of course. For one thing, the brain is many times more powerful, in most respects, than the most powerful computers we have yet created. Even though the adult human brain weighs only about sixteen hundred grams, about three pounds, and looks more like a lump of gray cauliflower than a desktop computer, the brain functions in some important ways much like the man-made computers which are patterned after it.

In non-technical language, a computer has three basic parts: a "video" screen, a keyboard, and a program disk. The *screen* is what we use to visually display what we are programming into the computer. The screen also displays the results—the words, numbers, or pictures that we want the computer to store or compute for us.

The *keyboard*, much like a typewriter keyboard, is what we use to type in the directions and information we give to the computer. And the *disk* (in a personal computer it's generally called a "floppy disk") is a small sheet of magnetic recording tape onto which we record the information. Whatever we record or program onto that disk will stay there forever unless someone changes it by erasing the old information and leaving it blank, or by typing in new information.

Each of us, along with our brain, has similar parts. In us, the computer's video screen is comparable to our appearance and our actions—what we "display" to the world around us.

In a human being, the computer keyboard is the same as our five senses. Anything we hear, see, taste, touch, smell—or anything we say to ourselves—is "programmed" into our brain through our keyboard: our five senses.

A personal computer uses a "floppy disk" to record the program and the information which the keyboard feeds to it. In the human computer, the floppy disk is our *subconscious mind*. Everything we experience is recorded—programmed—into our subconscious minds.

If you understand computers, my simplified explanation will be obvious and easy to understand. If computers are alien to you, it is important only to understand that whatever is programmed into your own personal "mental" computer is *permanently* programmed. That is, whatever programming you have received up to now is just as important and just as permanent as any "program" which has been key-punched into the most powerful man-made computers.

THE CONTROL CENTER

To help simplify the complex process of how and why the programming of the human brain affects us as much as it does, let's take a quick, imaginary look into the brain's central control room. That is the part of the brain where commands are received and where all the orders are handed out—the part of the brain that makes us feel good, work hard, and get things done. Or when not so well directed, it makes us slow down, fear the outcome, and stop dead-still in our tracks.

Imagine standing in the control center of the brain, in front of a wall which is completely covered with literally tens of thousands of light switches, much like the light switches in our homes.

One section of switches controls our moods. Another section governs our health. Another group of switches controls our emotions, another our planning functions, another our hopes and dreams. Another section is responsible for how we act, how we move, sit, stand, walk, look, speak, react and respond. Everything about us—our memory, our judgment, our attitude, our fears, our creativity, logic, and spirit—is controlled by the switches in our mental control room.

When any command is transmitted to the control room, the proper directions are sent to the appropriate panels of switches. Within a fraction of a second, some of those switches are turned off or turned on.

Within the brain itself, a network of tens of billions of neurons, and electrochemical switches called neurotransmitters, telegraph messages to every part of the brain, selecting just the right section of switches, which in turn switches parts of us "on" and parts of us "off."

The brain's infinitesimally small chemical receiving centers respond to almost imperceptible electrochemical signals which deliver nearly unmeasurable but highly potent chemical substances to our brain, our central nervous system, and to our bodies—which in turn control or affect everything we do.

It is the brain's responsibility to take care of us. It does so by constantly monitoring our needs and directing the various parts of our systems to take the necessary action. The brain automatically responds to every one of our unconscious electrical/chemical mental and physical commands—those that are principally concerned with keeping us alive.

THE BIOCHEMICAL ELECTRICAL IMPULSES CALLED "THOUGHTS"

But the brain responds, also automatically, to another kind of command—another exceptionally compelling electrical impulse which also turns the switches in the brain on or off. Those electrical impulses, those special mental commands which direct and control us, are called *thoughts*.

Every thought we think, every conscious or unconscious thought we say to ourselves, is translated into electrical impulses which, in turn, direct the control centers in our brains to electrically *and chemically* affect and control every motion, every feeling, every action we take, every moment of every day.

Whatever "thoughts" you have programmed into

yourself, or have allowed others to program into you, are affecting, directing, or controlling everything about you. From the day we were born, we have received a staggering amount of programming. It would require an immense computer just to compute the number of individual pieces of information we receive from the world around us in just one year. Some of the programming is obvious, but much of it we are never even aware of receiving.

The obvious programs are those comments, questions, and statements which are made to us directly. We are told by our parents, and other adults, what we can and cannot do. We are told what we are good at and what we are not. We are told how we look. We are told what to expect, what to believe in, how to act, and what to do or not to do. Because, starting out as children, completely dependent on others, it is important to our survival to listen and to believe what others say, we learn to accept what others tell us—and we learn to believe it.

CHAPTER FIVE

We Learn to Believe

WHAT ADULTS TELL US as children has an incredibly important effect on us. It forms what we believe about most of what is going on around us and almost everything that we come to believe about ourselves.

I still remember the time when, as a grade-school student, I wanted more than anything I could think of to play a musical instrument and be a member of the school band. Along with ten or twelve other students from my school class, I decided to try out for the band. After being handed a completely alien musical instrument and trying to get it to make music in front of the band instructor, my class teacher, and the other students, I was dismissed.

I knew that I had not done well. But it was an hour later, after the last student of the day had performed, that I overheard the band director telling my class teacher that not only could I not play in the band, but I had no musical ability and would never be able to play a musical instrument! What incredible programming for a twelve-year-old boy who had his heart set on learning how to play!

It worked. I heard, from someone else, that I had no musical ability and I believed it. I accepted as *fact* that I had no musical talent and that I never would. It wasn't until years later that I finally got up enough courage to rent a piano, learn some notes, and play it secretly when no one was around to remind me that I could not play. I never did develop the skill I wanted. But I learned, after some twenty frustrating years, that our school band director was wrong. And I had believed him.

Here is another example, in the opposite. Young Michael, who at the age of six often visited the elderly gentleman next door for afternoon chats, was safely out of sight but within hearing distance at the top of the stairs one evening, ready for bed, when the neighbor stopped by. Little Michael overheard the old man tell his mother that Michael was very creative, and he knew that Mike would grow up to do things that were creative.

Today, decades later, Mike Vance has been Dean of Walt Disney University, and more recently, through his personal consulting and his work with major corporations and organizations throughout the world, has gone on to become perhaps the premier creativity trainer in the United States today! Little Michael, by accident, overheard one small "program" about himself. And little Michael believed it.

Unfortunately, little of our own programming has done as much on our behalf. Can you imagine the number of times some child has heard the innocent but thoughtless words, "you'll never amount to much," or was told "that sport," "that career," "that mate," or "that dream" was not *right* for him or her? Just imagine what our eager and open young minds percieved and believed.

UNCONSCIOUS CONDITIONING
FROM OTHERS

Some of our programming is obvious. It stands up, gets our attention and demands our response. But much of our programming is not nearly so apparent. Most of it has been much more subtle.

Every day each of us receives an endless stream of commands, directives, controls, inducements, and expectations from others. Everything around us nudges, demands, or persuades. Even as adults we are met with a torrent of influences, most of which we are not even aware. We are ships with countless captains, all seeking to direct us on their own courses, for their own purposes, not even knowing they are leading our ships astray.

As long as you and I allow others to program us in a way that fits *their* choosing, we are, without a doubt, out of control, captive to the whims of some unknown destiny, not quite recognizing that what hangs in the balance is the fulfillment of our own futures.

Why do so many therapists regress their patients to a time in their childhood when the problem was created? Because that is where the beliefs began. That is where the fear, the trauma, or the self-identity first began to take hold. Out of those early years, each of us formed a composite picture of ourselves. It made little difference whether the pictures of ourselves which we created were true or not. Our experiences, our acceptance of what we heard from others and what we told ourselves became the foundation for the mental programming which directs us today.

Of course, not all of our past programming has been the wrong kind. Some of it has been very good. Most of us have experienced the love and caring of others. And most of us have been touched from time to time with visions of positive self-belief. We have had parents who countered their misgivings with encouragement. We have had coaches, teachers, and friends who expected the best. As we grew, all of us, from time to time, have had our successes.

At our best, we have been living with only a part of our life's programs working *for* us. Imagine what you could do if you could override the programs in your subconscious mind, those that still work against you, and replace them with a refreshing *new* program of absolute belief; an almost unconscious, automatic new program that would go to work for you—replacing the barriers with a refreshing new look at the life you have in front of you.

I once asked a woman who had lost a hundred and twenty pounds what she felt like after succeeding in her goal to lose the weight. Her answer was, "I feel like I've lost a hundred and twenty pounds!" I understood her joy. Sometime, when you are at a health spa or gymnasium, go over to the weight-lifting section and try to pick up a hundred and twenty pounds! Imagine losing, even for one day, all of the extra weight of self-doubt and disbelief we carry with us. Think how fast you could run! Think what you could do, beginning tomorrow, if the shackles of bad habits, old conditioning, and self-doubt were suddenly gone!

As you may have guessed, I haven't led you this far only to tell you that this kind of freedom is impossible or beyond the reach of any of us. Not only can you achieve that freedom for yourself, but we are about to see that there are a few, practical steps you can take to make the freedom of a self-directed mind a permanent part of every day of your life.

You already have all of the necessary equipment. You were born with everything you needed to live your life in a most exceptional and worthwhile way. It makes no difference what you have thought or what you have done in the past. From this day on, you can, if you choose, change a little to gain a lot.

YOUR PERSONAL ON-BOARD COMPUTER

Earlier we discussed how much of the programming which each of us received was the wrong kind; that as much as seventy-five percent or more of everything that is recorded and stored in our subconscious minds is counterproductive and works against us—in short, we are programmed *not* to succeed!

Let's say that I called you this evening and told you that I had just chartered a 747 airplane to go to Europe, and I was inviting you and your family or friends to join me! We are all going to fly to Europe for a fabulous two-week vacation (all expenses paid, of course!).

But now let's say that just as we are boarding the plane, we overhear the navigator talking to the captain. We hear him tell the captain that the on-board computer—the computer that flies the plane—is *programmed wrong;* it has been programmed so that seventy-five percent of the directions that will control the plane are the wrong directions!

If you knew that the airplane's on-board computer

was programmed wrong, what would you do next? You would get *off* the plane! You certainly wouldn't want to be on an airplane with a bad computer program. You would know that the plane would have to do one of two things: it would either land in the wrong place (not a happy thought while flying over the Atlantic) or it would *crash!*

And that is exactly the kind of program most of us have. No wonder things don't work! No wonder we dream, hope, try, struggle, get by, fall short of the mark or fail! No wonder we would like to get more out of life, solve some problems, or reach some goals—but can't seem to be able to. We've got a *bad* program! *We have been trying to achieve our goals with our own on-board computer pre-programmed to hold us back!*

Do you want to live with a bad program? Do you want to go through the rest of your life literally at the mercy of a program you don't want? You don't have to. You can override almost any conditioning you have ever received, in any part of your life. It makes absolutely no difference who, where, what, why, or how you have been in the past. It makes no difference what you believed about yourself or what others may have believed about you. It makes no difference what circumstances life may have tossed in your lap. You can put yourself in control. Now it's your turn.

You can *re*program. You can erase the old negative, counter-productive, work-against-you programming and replace it with a healthy, new, positive, *productive* kind of programming. And it's easy. *Erase and replace.* All you have to do is learn how to talk to yourself.

A NEW SET OF DIRECTIONS

If we change our attitudes and our behavior just by changing our programming, then none of us have to continue struggling through life with our old, negative programming dragging us down or holding us back. If we can just learn to give specific, productive new directions to our minds, then we have a chance to make things work—and keep working.

When I recognized that we could make a change in our lives by making a change in our programming, I saw for the first time, a crack in the wall of the 148,000 negatives, doubts, and destructive disbeliefs that each of us had built up in front of us. I began to believe that what was holding us back, defeating us, could itself be defeated. I began to realize that an exciting new future was about to become available to anyone who was standing behind the wall, waiting to get through.

What an exciting decision it is to break through that wall. Any of us can do it. Once we recognize what the real wall is, we can get past it.

CHAPTER SIX

The Wall

ALL OF US talk to ourselves all of the time. Our self-talk may be in spoken words or unspoken thoughts. It can take the form of feelings, impressions, or even wordless physical responses, the clutch in the stomach that comes when we are surprised or afraid, or the rush that comes with excitement or joy. We are thinking machines that never shut down. From childhood on we have been watching, listening to, sifting, sorting, analyzing, judging, cataloging, and storing everything that goes on about us.

Most of our self-talk is unconscious; we are not even aware of it. At times our self-talk comes in feelings that can't quite be put into words. At other times it comes in little flashes, flickers of thoughts which never quite catch fire or glow bright enough or last long enough to become ideas, clearly thought out and understood.

All of our thoughts, all of the pictures in our minds, are always tied to something else that we already know about. If you are given a new thought or a new picture, one you have never thought about or imagined before, your brain will immediately find something else in your mind to tie the new information to, to give it sense, to help you understand.

Every new thought you think has to have some old thoughts to stick to, a proper place to fit. When you are told something new, your brain will, in a fraction of a second, scan through literally millions of mental filing cabinets, filled with every idea or thought or impression you have ever stored. In that same fraction of a second, based on the information already stored in your mental files, your brain will send you an instant telegram, telling you how to feel about this new thought, where it should get filed, and whether you should accept it, believe it, keep it and use it, or disapprove, disbelieve, and throw it out.

The more we believe about something, the more we will accept other ideas which are similar. The more files we have in our mental filing cabinets, which tell us something about ourselves, the more we will attract and accept other thoughts and ideas which support and prove what is already stored in our files. The more you think about yourself in a certain way, the more you will think about yourself *in that same certain way!* The more you think about *anything* in a certain way, the more you will believe that *that* is how it really is. The mind works that way because the brain always tries to tie any *new* thing you think to something you already believe.

Understanding that makes it easy to understand why it is hard to teach old dogs new tricks, change our minds, or unstick us from the ideas we are solidly stuck in. It also tells us why the longer you believe something, the harder it is to change that belief. *The longer you have bought the thought, the "truer" it is.*

In our mental control centers we fill to overflowing the files that support what we have told ourselves most, and we throw out anything that disagrees. And meanwhile, we keep ourselves busily, blissfully ignorant of something about us that could have made a difference in our lives; something about ourselves called *the truth*.

A SELF-MADE WALL OF
NEGATIVE SELF-TALK

Throughout the years of solution-seeking in my quest for a more practical path to lasting self-improvement, I noticed that while most self-talk is either unconscious or goes unnoticed, some self-talk was glaringly obvious and, not surprisingly, clearly self-defeating. Although some of the Self-Talk I heard people using was constructive and beneficial, most of it was the opposite—the kind of self-talk that was counter-productive and self-defeating.

Each time I heard an example of this kind of "negative" self-talk, I wrote it down. In time, my list included hundreds of self-talk statements that are made by people—every day. Most of the people who use negative self-talk are not aware of what they are saying. And few, if any of them, are aware of the power of the programming—the *negative* programming—they are giving themselves.

If everything you tell yourself *about yourself* becomes a directive to your subconscious mind, then any time you make a statement about yourself that is negative you are directing your subconscious mind to make you become the person you just described—negatively!

Here are just a few examples of frequently used *negative* self-talk. As you read them, see if you know someone who says something similar, or if you have said something like any of these yourself:

I can't remember names.
It's going to be another one of those days!
It's just no use!
I just know it won't work!
Nothing ever goes right for me.
That's just my luck.
I'm so clumsy!
I don't have the talent.
I'm just not creative.
Everything I eat goes right to my waist.
I can't seem to get organized.
Today just isn't my day!
I can never afford the things I want.
I already know I won't like it.
No matter what I do I can't seem to lose weight.
I never have enough time.
I just don't have the patience for that.
That really makes me mad!
Another blue Monday!
When will I ever learn!
I get sick just thinking about it.
Sometimes I just hate myself.
I'm just no good!
I'm too shy.
I never know what to say.
With my luck I don't have a chance!
I'd like to stop smoking but I can't seem to quit.
Things just aren't working out right for me.

WHAT TO SAY WHEN YOU TALK TO YOUR SELF

I don't have the energy I used to.
I'm really out of shape.
*I never have any money left over at the end of
    the month.*
Why should I try, it's not going to work anyway!
I've never been any good at that.
My desk is always a mess!
The only kind of luck I have is bad luck!
I never win anything!
I fell like I'm over the hill.
Someone always beats me to it!
Nobody likes me.
I never get a break!
It seems like I'm always broke!
Everything I touch turns to bleep.
Nobody wants to pay me what I'm worth.
Sometimes I wish I'd never been born!
I'm just no good at math.
I lose weight but then I gain it right back again.
I get so depressed!
I just can't seem to get anything done!
Nothing seems to go right for me!
I'm just not a salesman.
That's impossible!
There's just no way!
I always freeze up in front of a group.
*I'm nothing without my first cup of coffee in the
    morning.*
I just can't get with it today.
I'll never get it right!
I just can't take it anymore!
I hate my job.
I get a cold this time every year.
I'm just not cut out for that.
I'm really at the end of my rope.

You can't trust anyone anymore!
I just can't handle this!
I never seem to get anyplace on time.
I've always been bad with words.
If only I were smarter.
If only I were taller.
If only I had more time.
If only I had more money.
. . . and on, and on, and on.

Imagine sitting down at your personal computer keyboard and typing any one of those directions into the computer. And imagine that your computer will do whatever you program it to do.

That is exactly what we do to our personal computers! No wonder things go wrong! No wonder things don't work out right! If your personal computer—the one that flies your plane—is programmed with the wrong information, *you cannot possibly be as successful as you would like to be*—you cannot get where you want to go!

LIVING WITH THE RESULTS

One day I was having lunch with a friend of mine who is a motivational speaker and author. We were sitting in a coffee shop located in a large Las Vegas convention hotel. While we were waiting for our lunch, we were discussing negative self-talk and commenting on how we end up becoming the result of what we say to ourselves. During our discussion a perfect example of just that happened.

As our waitress approached our table with both arms laden with plates of food, she stumbled and dropped an armload of hot food on the table and floor in front of us, and exclaimed loudly, "Oh, I'm *so clumsy!*"

My friend and I had just witnessed a firsthand example of the result of the simplest kind of negative self-talk. I do not know how many times before that waitress had told herself she was clumsy. But she had undoubtedly said it to herself often enough to believe that it was true, and to make it happen!

As another example, let's take something as common as the problem of not being able to remember names. For twenty-five years you may have said to yourself, "I can never remember names." Then one evening you go to a party. You are introduced to someone whose name you want to remember and you say to yourself, "I'm going to remember this person's name." What happens ten seconds later? You forget the name! Why? Because for the past twenty-five years you have been telling yourself that that's what you'll do. You have been *programming* yourself to forget!

Minutes later, at the party, you find yourself standing there, a little embarrassed, mentally going through the alphabet, trying to remember the person's name. And meanwhile, while you're feeling forgetful and foolish, your subconscious, feeling very proud, is saying, "*See, I did what you told me to! I made you forget the name!*"

If your self-talk, the directions you give to your subconscious mind, will do that, don't you suppose it will do whatever else you tell it to do? If you were to reprogram someone strongly enough for them to believe that it was safe to drive up to an intersection, and turn the wrong way into oncoming traffic, they would do it! *The human brain will do anything possible you tell it to do if you tell it often enough and strongly enough!* If you tell it the wrong thing about yourself, that is what it will accept—and act upon!

The subconscious mind does not see the difference between the statement that we are clumsy and the statement that we are graceful, well-coordinated, and in control. It does not know the difference between being told that we are poor, and the statement that we are wealthy. It accepts our programming just as we give it.

Our internal programming mechanism treats anything we tell it with equal indifference. As a result, when we casually state, "No matter what I do, I just can't seem to make enough money to make ends meet," our subconscious mind says, "Okay, I'll do what you're telling me to do. I'll make sure you can't make ends meet." In turn, it will unleash its powerful control over our mental and physical selves to achieve the result it was told to accomplish.

I met a gentleman, recently, who I would consider to be a fine man, but unfortunate. After twenty years of marriage, raising several children into their teens, and building a profitable business, he lost his wife to divorce, his children to the wife, and his business to his partners. What intrigued me about this man's story was that he talked only of his failures, his defeats, his downfall, and the problems he anticipated for his future. It was sad to see someone with his depth, his warmth, and his capabilities completely subjected to the failures he had long ago created for himself in his own mind.

As was the case with that individual, through a complex process of electrochemical physiological controls, our personal computer will affect and influence what we do in every area of our lives. It will directly affect everything about us, from how we get along with someone at home, to the amount of money we earn.

A typical example of this is our own self-accepted beliefs about our personal financial capabilities—or limitations. Unless we change the program we gave to ourselves, the one that told us we can't seem to earn enough money, our subconscious will successfully accomplish its programmed task of keeping us earning less than we would like. Had we given it the right programming, that same subconscious mind, instead of keeping us poor or of average means, would just as gladly have made us rich.

CHAPTER SEVEN

Passing It On

BECAUSE WE LEARNED our programs from people around us, it is natural that we also pass the same kind of programming on to others. Unless we learn differently, we end up giving the same programming to our own children. I have collected dozens of examples of statements and comments which loving parents have told their children without once realizing that they were creating a self-belief in that child that would create *failure* instead of the happiness and success they were trying to bestow.

You may recognize some of these examples. Sincere, loving, caring parents, teachers, and friends have told children: *"You're just no good at that," "Your room is always a mess," "Can't you do anything right?" "You're just like your father!"* (which always seems to be said when the child has done something wrong), *Why can't you be more like your sister (or brother)?" "You'll never be an artist (or athlete, etc.)," "You just don't try!" "You never listen to me," "I tell you to do something and you do just the opposite!" "You never study," "Your grades are atro-*

cious," "You talk too much," "You always hang around with the wrong kind of friends," "You don't even know where home is anymore," "You're lazy," "You don't care about anyone but yourself," "You're determined to cause problems," "You just don't think," etc., etc., etc. And some children, even while you are reading this, are being told the most assuredly destructive words, "You'll never amount to anything."

I suspect that some of what is said to children and teenagers behind closed doors may be even stronger than the few examples I have just given. But with that kind of programming, even in its most innocent and casual form, can you imagine how many times young, impressionable, unknowing children are told things which end up working against them—how many times we type a *bad* program into their personal computers?

Of course, much of what we say is said for the purpose of giving a child proper training, a proper "upbringing." But in so doing, by using words which program the child in the wrong way, we unwittingly help the child create a self-identity which believes that what we are saying is "the truth"—we create a picture portrait of how the child sees himself or herself inside, and eventually will become.

Think for a moment of the dreams you *know* you could have accomplished in your own life, think of the talents and skills already within you which could have been developed into lasting achievements had you just had the right amount of self-belief—the belief that you *could* instead of the belief that you could *not*. Most of us, if given a magic wand, which when waved could fulfill any of our dreams, would most certainly make some changes in our lives.

All of us have had the dreams. All of us deserve to

see our dreams come true. Were it not for the brick wall of bad programming that stands in our way, each of us, each day, would be living out more of those dreams, reaching heights of attainment we seldom even dream of.

We are fortunate to be living at a time when we are beginning to understand what goes on inside that incredible mechanism we call a brain. By unlocking even a few of the secrets about our minds, we have learned that we have a *personal* vote in the outcome of our own destinies.

We have learned that what we put into our brains is what we will get back out. We also have learned that the subconscious mind is a sponge—it will believe anything you tell it—it will even believe a lie—if you tell it often enough and strongly enough. The brain makes no moral judgments, it simply accepts what you tell it. The desk-top computer at the office doesn't care what is programmed into it. It never questions whether you are telling it the truth or not. It just accepts and acts upon whatever you program into it. It makes no difference whether the things you have told yourself or believed about yourself in the past were true or not. *The brain doesn't care!*

THE MACHINE THAT NEVER SLEEPS

Your subconscious mind is working right now, day and night, to make sure that you become precisely the person you have *unconsciously* described yourself to be. If your program pictures you as having trouble earning enough income, your subconscious mind is doing everything it can, right now, to make sure that you have trouble earning more money. If you have conditioned yourself to believe that you can't stick to a diet, you can be sure that your subconscious mind will make *sure* that no diet will work for you—at least not for long! Your subconscious can only do for you what you (and others) tell it to do.

In a previous chapter I said that during the formative years of our lives, each of us is told "no," or what we *cannot* do, tens of thousands of times. Each of those "cannots" was a directive to our subconscious minds. And as we, because of our conditioning, began to follow suit and say similar cannots to ourselves, we fell into the unconscious habit of programming ourselves in the same wrong way as did our parents, friends, and others around us. And right now, at this moment, each of our subconscious minds is working to make sure we become just as those tens of thousands of negative directives programmed us to be.

Since that time, of course, we have continued to give ourselves new programs. The examples of negative statements I gave you earlier are only a few leaves in a forest of negative self-talk. In fact, most of our average, habit-formed, everyday self-talk is the kind that we don't even notice. It is the kind that we say to ourselves silently, often without words. Much of our self-talk is made up of the quiet nudges of self-doubt, the unspoken fears of little (or grand) failures, and the nagging discomfort of knowing that things aren't right.

When we talk to our friends, it sometimes seems easier to talk about problems than about exciting potentials. Our daily conversation scripts often sound like they were written by the same editors who design the front page of the morning paper. We live, in our poorly programmed unconscious minds, in the disquieting shadow-world of uncertainty—believing that we should be achieving, but not knowing why, after so much frustration and trying, we are not.

By the time most of us reach adulthood, we are so conditioned to think in a certain way that our pattern of self-talk becomes habit. It is fixed. And for most, it remains that way. How we look at life, what we believe about ourselves, how we view *anything,* and what we do about it, gets filtered through our preconceptions.

We have told ourselves over and over, consciously and unconsciously, what does not work. In the past, too often we learned to automatically believe *the worst first, and the best last.* But now we have learned that it does not have to be that way. There is something, starting right now, that you can do about it. It is the key to how you manage yourself, and how you live and manage the rest of your life.

CHAPTER EIGHT

The Self-Management Sequence

THERE IS A natural process by which success or failure in managing or controlling our lives takes place. The process consists of a sequence of steps. If we are aware of what the steps are, we can improve our chances and accelerate our advances. If we are not aware of what is causing our success, or foiling it, we end up at the mercy of chance. Life is not a matter of luck or fortune. We are not playing our lives out at a gaming table. If we leave our lives up to chance, chances are, we'll fail.

That is because success in self-management is always the *result* of something else, something that leads up to it. Now, we know that there are times when it looks like something good that happens is just an "accident." But there are those who would argue that *nothing* ever happens by accident—that everything that occurs in our lives does so because of what we mentally "create" to happen. Most of what seems to happen *to* you, happens because *of* you—something you created, directed, influenced, or allowed to happen.

Let's take your personal successes or failures on an average. Whether you are examining your smaller, everyday achievements, or the bigger monthly or yearly successes, by and large, on the average, those achievements and successes were not accidental. They were the result of something else.

The same is true of those things you did which didn't work out so well. On the average, the failures, too, were the results of something else—and that something else, in most cases, whether you succeeded or failed—was *you!* Something you did (or did not do) was the cause of that success or failure. Here's how it works.

THE SELF-MANAGEMENT SEQUENCE: THE FIVE STEPS THAT CONTROL OUR SUCCESS OR FAILURE

1. *BEHAVIOR*

The step that most *directly* controls our success or failure is our behavior—what we do or do not do. Behavior means our *actions*. How we act, what we do, each moment of each day will determine whether or not we will be successful that moment or that day in anything that we do. The right series of the right actions will always end up making things work better than the wrong series of the wrong actions. In most cases, if you do the right thing, you're going to achieve the right results.

This step involves even the simplest level of behavior. As an example, if you like your job, do the right thing at the right time, and keep at it, there is a good chance that your job will do well for you. If, on the other hand, you do not like your work and do things which work against you on the job, it won't work as well for you.

Let's use another example. If a student in school refuses to study, never pays attention, and misses a lot of classes (all behavior), will the student do well in school? Probably not. If that student behaves in a way that says "I don't like being where I am," his or her behavior will ultimately cause a problem. The good grades won't show up and if something doesn't change, eventually neither will the student.

The same is true of your home life. If you don't like where you are in your home life, what will you do? If you are like most of us, in one way or another, your behavior, your actions will alert those around you that you are unhappy. The result will be an unhappy home life, or at a minimum you will have to live with disagreements, arguments, and unhappiness in one form or another.

On the other hand, if your actions are those which work *for* you instead of against you, the likelihood is that things around you will have a better chance of working for you instead of against you.

But it goes far beyond that. How you manage yourself, what you do, how you act, each and every moment, every word you speak, motion you make, and action you take, or do not take, will determine how well anything in your life works for you. It does not take a wizard to tell us that when we do the *right* things, there is always a better chance that things will work better for us than when we do the *wrong* things.

But why do we do what we do? Why do we *not* do the things we know we should, and so often say and do things that we know we should *not?* What makes us do what we do? What makes us act the way we act, behave the way we behave? Why do we ever do *anything* that works against us instead of always doing exactly that which works *for* us? Is it because we don't know any better? No. We usually know what's right and what's wrong.

The reason we don't heed even our own advice is because of something else which affects, directs, influences, or controls all of our actions. That something that makes us do what we do is called our:

2. *FEELINGS*

Every action we take is first filtered through our feelings. How we *feel* about something will always determine or affect what we *do* and how well we do it.

If we feel good or positive about something, we will behave more positively about it. Our feelings will directly influence our actions. Have you ever watched a child who was made to eat something he didn't like? How did he act? I've seen children who looked as though they were going to die right there on the spot! But set a favorite dessert in front of the same child and what will he do? He may look as though he's going to dive into it head first!

What is the difference between the one plate of food and the other? It's *not* that one type of food is better than the other. The difference is in how the child has come to *feel* about the food. The way the child felt determined what action he took. In one instance he fought it, in the other he relished it.

I have a friend whose worst fear is that of flying. Ordinarily she is levelheaded and possesses an even disposition. But because of her fear of being in an airplane, she would rather drive a car from her home in the Midwest to visit her family on the East Coast, and lose two or three days getting there, than hop on a plane and be with her family in two or three short hours. When circumstances demand that she does fly, she loses her well-mannered, even temperament, her stress level triples, her anxieties take over, and she gets sick even before the flight begins.

Is it the flying? No. It is her *feelings* about flying that cause her to act the way she does. In this example, you'll notice that, once again, it made no difference if the individual's feelings were "rational"; her feelings nonetheless directly controlled, influenced, and severely affected the woman's actions.

Your feelings about anything you do will affect how you do it. It doesn't have to be feelings of like or dislike, joy or fear; *all* of your feelings affect your actions. How you feel about your job, your mate, your family, money, your health, your self, your success, will determine how you behave in each of these areas. If your feelings are positive and productive, your actions will follow.

But what causes you to *have* the feelings which are so much a part of you? Did you get them by accident? What creates the way you feel about anything? Chance? Never. Your feelings are created, controlled, determined, or influenced by your:

WHAT TO SAY WHEN YOU TALK TO YOUR SELF

3. *ATTITUDES*

Your attitudes are the perspectives from which you view life. Some people seem to have a good attitude about most things. Some people seem to have a bad attitude about everything. But when you look closer, you will find that most of us have a combination of attitudes, some good, some not so good.

Whatever attitude we have about anything will affect how we feel about it, which in turn determines how we'll act about it and that in turn determines whether or not we will do well. So our attitudes play a very important part in helping us become successful.

In fact, as we can see, a good attitude is *essential* to achievement of any kind! We so often hear of someone who is said to have a "bad attitude." The term is often applied to young people, especially to teenagers who frequently get into trouble, but we often hear it about adults, too. The implication is always that the individual in question is not going to make it if he doesn't change his attitude.

I would agree. Without a good attitude, a perspective which allows one to see the opportunities ahead and set his sights to reach them, he never will. But even more important is the fact that in order to possess the kinds of feelings which work *for* us, we've got to have the right attitudes to start with!

But where do we get our attitudes? Are we born with them? Or do they just appear out of nowhere?

Our attitudes are no accident. They don't just *happen*. Our attitudes are created, controlled, or influenced entirely by our:

4. *BELIEFS*

What we *believe* about anything will determine our attitudes about it, create our feelings, direct our actions, and in each instance, help us to do well or poorly, succeed or fail. The belief that we have about anything is so powerful that it can even make something appear to be something *different* than what it really is! "Belief" does not require that something be the way we see it to be. It only requires us to believe that it is.

Belief does not require something to be true. It only requires us to *believe that it's true!* That's powerful stuff! That means most of what reality is, to each of us, is based on what we have come to believe—whether it's true or not!

It is possible that tomorrow morning, in some classroom in the Soviet Union, there will sit a little boy or girl who believes that the United States is bad. It is also likely that tomorrow morning, in some classroom in the United States, there will sit a young boy or girl who believes that the Soviet Union is bad. It makes no difference whether it is true or not. It is what they believe. And what they believe will affect their attitudes, feelings, and actions. One day when they grow older, they could shoot at each other. To each of them it would be right. It would be what they believe.

When I was a child, sitting on a church bench, trying to understand what the man in the pulpit was talking about, I remember him telling us to "believe." I didn't know how to do that. I thought that some people were lucky and some were not. Some just naturally got to believe and some didn't. I did not know yet where belief comes from, and I certainly didn't know the power that belief would have in my life and the power beliefs had held in the lives of every human being who ever had lived.

As an example of how important belief can be, imagine believing something about yourself, something that was working against you, but was not true.

Let's say that you believed that you had trouble making friends easily, or being accepted easily and naturally by others. You believed that you took a social back seat to people who seemed to be more popular. As a result, you found yourself standing back at social gatherings, self-conscious and unsure of what to say. At your work you often missed opportunities because you did not speak up—even when your idea was better than the idea that was accepted from someone else who did speak up. Let's say that you knew that you wanted to be intelligent and witty and fun, but you believed that the *outside* you just didn't measure up.

Since whatever you believe about yourself will end up affecting what you do, you can be sure that if you believe that you are not as socially successful as you would like to be, your *belief* about yourself will turn out to be correct—whether it was true or not. All social behavior is conditioned—no one is born popular and socially adept. Every social grace, skill, and comfort level that we have, successful or unsuccessful, is based on what we believe about ourselves. If you tell yourself that you can*not,* what can the only outcome be?

We all have thousands of big and little beliefs about ourselves. Some of them probably are true. I suspect that most of them are not. But your mind will act as though they are true if you believe them.

What makes us believe? Do our beliefs just one day

spring out of nowhere? Were our beliefs handed to us on the day of our births, like birthmarks of our heredities to be kept forever? Do we create them ourselves? Where do we get them? Our beliefs are not accidents of nature. Our beliefs are created and directed entirely by our:

5. *PROGRAMMING*

We believe what we are *programmed* to believe. Our conditioning, from the day we were born, has created, reinforced, and nearly permanently cemented most of what we believe about ourselves and what we believe about most of what goes on around us. Whether the programming was right or wrong, true or false, the result of it is what we believe.

It all starts with our programming! What we have accepted from the outside world, or fed to ourselves, has initiated a natural cause and effect chain reaction sequence which cannot fail to lead us to successful self-management, or to the unsuccessful mismanagement of ourselves, our resources, and our futures.

It is our programming that sets up our beliefs, and the chain reaction begins. In logical progression, what we believe determines our attitudes, affects our feelings, directs our behavior, and determines our success or failure:

1. *Programming creates beliefs.*

2. *Beliefs create attitudes.*

3. *Attitudes create feelings.*

    4.   *Feelings determine actions.*

    5.   *Actions create results.*

That's how the brain works. If you want to manage yourself in a better way, and change your results, you can do so at any time you choose. Start with the first step. Change your programming.

CHAPTER NINE

The Five Levels of Self-Talk

WHAT IS SELF-TALK and how does it work? The definition of Self-Talk can be simply stated: *Self-Talk is a way to override our past negative programming by erasing or replacing it with conscious, positive new directions*. Self-Talk is a practical way to live our lives by active intent rather than by passive acceptance.

With Self-Talk, we have a way to give new directions to our subconscious minds by talking to ourselves in a different way, consciously reprogramming our internal control centers with words and statements which are more effective, more helpful to every part of us that we would like to improve. The Self-Talk statements paint a new internal picture of ourselves as we would most *like* to be.

Self-Talk gives each of us a way to change what we would like to change, even if we haven't been able to do so in the past. It offers us the chance to stop being the old self and start to become a different, better self, a self which is no longer the product of conditioned response, but governed instead by personal choice.

Actually, there are several kinds of self-talk. Each

of us, each day, may use any of five different levels of self-talk. Each level is specific and distinct from the others. Some of the levels work for us and some work against us. The more you know about each of them, the faster and more easily you will be able to master using the *right* kind of Self-Talk for yourself.

LEVEL I SELF-TALK—
THE LEVEL OF
NEGATIVE ACCEPTANCE
("I can't . . .")

The five levels of self-talk start at the lowest, least beneficial level. At the bottom of the list—and the most harmful self-talk we can use—is Level I, the level of Negative Acceptance. That is self-talk by which you say something bad or negative about yourself, and you accept it.

Earlier we discussed several dozen commonly used self-talk statements and phrases. All of them were Level I self-talk. This level is easy to spot. It is most always characterized by the words, "*I can't . . .*" or "if only I could . . ." or "I wish I could, but I can't," and so on. All Level I self-talk works against us. And unfortunately, it is the most frequently used self-talk of all!

"I just don't have the energy I used to," "I could never do that," "I just can't seem to lose weight," "Well . . . I just don't know . . .," "Today's just not my day," and "I just can't!," are typical of the kinds of doubts, fears, misgivings, and hesitations we program ourselves with when we say any Level I self-talk phrase to ourselves, out loud, silently, or to someone else. Remember, the subconscious mind is listening and waiting for our instructions, and it doesn't care what we tell it; it just does it!

Level I self-talk represents everything from our simplest misgivings to the worst fears we have about ourselves. It is our way of telling ourselves to hesitate, question our capabilities, and accept less than we know we could have done, had we only given ourselves a chance. It is our way of timidly hiding in the shadows instead of boldly thriving in the sunshine.

There is no way to estimate the amount of havoc and misdirection that Level I self-talk wreaks in our lives. It clutters, blocks, and confuses. It turns self-assurance into self-doubt and chaos. It cripples our best intentions and seduces us into becoming satisfied with mediocrity. It is the heart of a "get by" attitude, its subtle whispers telling us to passively accept a fate far less great than we had once dreamed of attaining. It is the mythical Siren which draws us onto the shore, dashing our hopes on reefs of despair and complacency.

Imagine going through your life using that kind of self-talk on yourself! When you think about it, why would anyone (once they know) want to use any self-talk that would program them to fail or do less than they could? Yet, that is exactly what most of us have done.

It makes no difference how harmless the words seem at the time, they are the backbone of everything which works against us and stands in our way. Rid yourself of the negative "I can'ts" of Level I self-talk, and you will have rid yourself of your greatest foe.

LEVEL II SELF-TALK—
THE LEVEL OF *RECOGNITION,*
AND NEED TO CHANGE
(*"I need to . . . I should . . ."*)

This level is beguiling. On the surface it looks as though it should work *for* us. But instead, it works against us! In this level of self-talk we are stating to ourselves and to others our recognition of our need to change.

Level II self-talk is characterized by words such as, "I need to . . .," or "I ought to . . .," or "I should. . . ." Why does that work against us? Because it recognizes a problem, but creates no solution. When you say to yourself (or to someone else), "I really need to get more organized," what are you really saying? You are saying, "I really need to get more organized . . . *but I'm not!"* When you complete the sentence, it is always, unconsciously, ended with an unspoken, but still programmed, Level I statement of *negative* self-talk!

"I really should try to get to work on time." "I've just got to lose some weight!" "I really need to cut down on my smoking." "I've got to do something about that!" "I really ought to take more time with my kids." "I know I should study harder." Anytime you hear yourself telling yourself any Level II self-talk, stop for a moment and *complete the sentence*—finish, out loud, the program you are actually directing to your subconscious mind.

Your self-talk then becomes, "I'd really like to earn more income . . . *but I'm not! I wish I could . . . but I can't!* I know I need to take care of that . . . *but I'm not taking care of it*. I ought to call home more often . . . *but I don't*. I'd like things to work out better . . . *but they won't!"*

Those are the directives we unwittingly give to ourselves. Those are the seemingly innocent but exceptionally effective programs we feed to the most powerful control center known to man. Instead of giving birth to dreams and accomplishment, Level II self-talk creates guilt, disappointment, and an acceptance of our own self-imagined inadequacies. Is that good programming? No, it is not. Will it help us succeed? No, it will not.

LEVEL III SELF-TALK—
THE LEVEL OF
DECISION TO CHANGE
("I never . . . I no longer . . .")

Level III Self-Talk is the first level of Self-Talk that works *for* you instead of against you. In this level you recognize the need to change, but also you make the decision to do something about it—and you state the decision in the "present tense"—as though the change has already taken place.

Level III is characterized by the words, "I never . . .," or "I no longer." In this level you say, "I never smoke!" "I no longer have a problem dealing with people at work." "I never eat more than I should." "I never get upset in traffic." "I no longer put off doing anything I want to get done." When you move to Level III, you are automatically beginning to rephrase old negative "cannots," putting them behind you, and stating them in a positive new way that tells your subconscious mind to wake up, get moving, and make the change.

When you begin to practice the new Self-Talk for yourself, you will find that you will need to use Level III Self-Talk only on those occasions when you are working at effecting a specific change.

Let's use the example of someone who smokes, but who really wants to quit. If you have been a smoker, and want to quit, you may want to try this yourself. Let's say that you smoke, but you finally decide that you want to stop smoking for good. So you begin by using Level III Self-Talk. You say to yourself, "I never smoke!" "I no longer enjoy smoking and I have quit." You use your new Self-Talk silently to yourself, but you also say it out loud, even when you are with other people. Until now, when you felt like lighting a cigarette, you would simply do so, think nothing about it, and say nothing about it.

But now, when you light a cigarette, you say out loud, "I never smoke." The first thing that will happen is that if you say those words in front of someone else, while you are lighting your cigarette, your friends are going to think you're a little strange! But you continue to say the words, both to yourself and out loud. And for a while, you continue to smoke, just as you have become conditioned to smoking, but you also continue to give yourself new Self-Talk at the same time—"I never smoke . . . I no longer smoke . . .," etc.

In not too long a time, what will happen? One day you will be lighting a cigarette and saying "I never smoke," and your subconscious mind is going to say, "Then what are you doing with that little white thing in your hand? . . . And one end of it is on *fire!*" You have been giving new programming to your subconscious, telling yourself that you no longer need to smoke. And your subconscious mind will *automatically* react by making sure that you no longer smoke! That's what you have started telling it to do!

There is, of course, more to Self-Talk than just a few simple words. Many habits, including smoking, have been years in the making and require a solid program of new Self-Talk to break them down and replace them. (How to do that is discussed in a later chapter.)

It doesn't make any difference that you're still a smoker when you start telling your subconscious that you no longer smoke. Remember, the subconscious mind will believe anything you tell it if you tell it long enough and strongly enough. It will simply go to work to carry out its new directives. Your subconscious mind will receive the new direction, create a new, non-smoking picture of you in your control center, and convince you to put the cigarette out. You no longer smoke! That's exactly what you told your subconscious mind; that's exactly what it will do. When the new programming takes over it won't be the result of magic, hypnosis, meditation, or luck. That's just the way the mind works. It works because you tell it what to do. Learn to tell it in the right way, and it will do it.

LEVEL IV—THE LEVEL OF
THE BETTER YOU
("I am . . .")

This is the most effective kind of Self-Talk we can ever use. In our Self-Talk vocabularies, Level IV is the kind of Self-Talk that has been used the least and is needed most. It is at this level that you are painting a completed new picture of yourself, the way you really wanted to be, handing it to your subconscious, and saying, "*This* is the me I want you to create! Forget all that bad programming I gave you in the past. This is your new program. Now let's get to work at it!"

Level IV Self-Talk is characterized by the words, "I am . . ." "I am organized and in control of my life. I am a winner! I am healthy, energetic, enthusiastic, and I'm going for it! Nothing can stop me now. I like who I am. I am in tune, on top, and in touch. I have determination, drive, and self-belief. I am living the life I choose, and I choose what's right!" Now, the ex-smoker in Level IV would say, "I don't smoke! My lungs are clean and healthy. I have no habits which harm me or hold me back in any way."

Instead of struggling with the past Level I Self-Talk, the Level IV Self-Talker deals with problems and opportunities in a whole new, productive, *self-activating* way: The past procrastinator, who had been programmed to put things off, now says, "I do everything I need to do when I need to do it. I enjoy getting things done and I enjoy doing things on time and in just the right way!" The past problem is turned around to begin creating ongoing daily success. Instead of saying, "I can never remember names," the Level IV Self-Talker automatically says, "I have a great memory! People are important to me and I am able to remember any name I choose to remember, anytime I want."

Level IV Self-Talk is the *positive Self-Talk* that is the opposite of Level I. It replaces helpless "cannots" with vibrant "Yes, I cans!" Level IV Self-Talk inspires, encourages, urges, and implores. It tugs at our hearts, touches our hopes, and paints in the pictures that color our dreams. It excites, demands, and pushes us forward. It strengthens the armor of our spirit and hardens the steel of our determination. This is the Self-Talk that challenges us to do battle with our fears and end up the victor. It is the Self-Talk which stirs us to action, fills us up with self-belief, and plants our feet firmly on the solid bedrock of success.

Name the adversary, state the problem, and you can find the self-talk that created it. But for every word of negative self-talk that has ever been uttered, there is the *right* kind of Self-Talk to counter it, reprogram, fix the problem, and make it right.

There are hundreds of examples, already written, of this special, powerful, reprogramming Level IV Self-Talk: *"I am a winner! I believe in myself. I respect myself and I like who I am. I have made the decision to win in my life and that's what I'm doing!"* Can you imagine going through the rest of your life with that kind of Self-Talk on your side? Think of the programming that kind of direction would create. It is yours for the taking. It is yours the moment you decide to choose a better way. You deserve the best out of life. Perhaps it's time to do something about it.

LEVEL V SELF-TALK—
THE LEVEL OF
UNIVERSAL AFFIRMATION
("It is . . .")

This level of Self-Talk has been spoken for thousands of years. It is as old as the ancient religions which inspired it. It is the Self-Talk of "oneness" with God. This level of Self-Talk speaks of a unity of spirit, a divine and timeless cosmic affinity which transcends all worldly things and gives meaning to our being. It is the language of those who, having conquered their ties to a life of earth-bound demands, choose to seek their manifest place in something greater—something beyond the ken of most others, but within the reach of their unearthly dreams. This is the Self-Talk for seekers, still living among mankind, but anxious to find a greater reward.

Level V Self-Talk is characterized by the words, "It is . . ." It sounds like this: "I am one with the universe and it is one with me. I am of it, within it, and exist as a shining spark in a firmament of divine goodness."

They are beautiful words, and they are meaningful. But lest I sound as though I am giving this level of Self-Talk less than its due, let me say only that those whose quest has placed them at this level already know. They don't need to read this book to learn that Self-Talk, to them, "affirmations," will serve as mantras to help them achieve their rather special goals.

It is still important, however, that we take care today of the things that are required today. So I urge you to begin to use the Self-Talk of Level III and Level IV. If it's right, Level V will come in due time. For now, learn the Self-Talk that will get you to work on time, help you fix your family ties, give yourself the self-image you deserve, and get the basic things in *this* life in order.

YOU CAN BEGIN RIGHT NOW

There are two levels of Self-Talk which you should learn first—and two others which you should *unlearn* fast. Starting right now, the moment you recognize why the self-talk you have used at Levels I and II *hasn't* worked, stop using it! There's no reason to use it any longer. Replace those two negative kinds of self-talk with the Self-Talk of Levels III and IV.

If you'd like to start working at it right now, reread the section on Level II and start learning Self-Talk for yourself. That's the Self-Talk that will get you going, change what you want to change, and get you headed on a journey that will take you toward the fulfillment of your dreams and away from the frustrating roadblocks that have been standing in your way. In a later chapter, you will be given step-by-step directions on how to start using the new Self-Talk automatically and unconsciously.

For now, just listen to anything you may be saying to yourself that could be working against you, *turn it around,* and start using the Self-Talk that works *for* you.

CHAPTER TEN

The Problem with Positive Thinking

THE CONCEPT OF positive thinking is one of the better ideas to come out of the self-help literature of this century. It is one of those potentially life-changing concepts, however, which sometimes seems to work better in theory than it does in practice. If you were to walk down the street today and ask the next ten people that you meet, "Do you believe in positive thinking?"—most of them would say "yes." Some would say, "I think it's a great idea! It doesn't work for me, but I know it works for other people." Positive thinking *should* work for everyone. But if it should, why doesn't it?

Literally millions of people have been helped by reading the great books on thinking positively. Many of those people, when they wanted to solve problems in their lives, turned to the pages of the books to find encouragement and solutions, and they found what they were looking for. I first read Dr. Peale's great book, *The Power of Positive Thinking,* when I was sixteen years old, and like many other of the book's readers, I found it was a book to be read more than once.

When I discuss positive thinking—what's right about it and what isn't—in seminars and training programs, I am invariably challenged by someone in the audience who is a devoted believer in the concept. How could I possibly question something that is so clearly *positive!?* After all, don't I teach a form of positive thinking myself?

The answer is that the popularly accepted form of positive thinking is an excellent concept that goes a long way toward helping people readjust their thinking and do better in their lives. It is one of the answers to helping us effect a major change in our lives. *Almost.* It takes us most of the way but not quite all of the way. That is like jumping ninety percent of the way across a chasm. We *almost* make it to the other side.

But just making a decision to never again think negatively, and for the rest of our lives think positively, while it may work for a time, can't last indefinitely. Why? Because the mental program which was already set up in our subconscious minds is the *old* kind of programming—the kind that is preprogrammed to *dis*believe new information which does not agree with the information already stored in the subconscious mind. If you tell yourself that from today onward you will never again think negatively, without at the same time giving yourself a specific, *new* word-for-word vocabulary of the *right* things to say, you will soon slip back into the comfortable old habit of thinking negatively.

That is why the decision to be a positive thinker is so often short-lived. It seems to be a great idea at the time; but too often it doesn't keep on working. I have known people who have become completely disillusioned about believing in anything positive, simply because they wanted to believe, tried "positive thinking" for a while, and then stopped. Their old program literally stopped it from working. When it didn't work, their disappointment led to the conviction that positive thinking is for dreamers, but not for them.

But positive thinking could work, *can* work, if the negative thoughts we are told to avoid are immediately replaced with the opposite.

YOUR MENTAL APARTMENT

Imagine for a moment a "mental apartment"—the place you live with your thoughts. That mental apartment is furnished with everything you think about yourself and the world around you; it is furnished with your thoughts. Much of the mental furniture in this mental apartment is "hand-me-down" furniture. It is the old negative way of thinking which was handed down to us from our parents, our friends, our teachers, and everyone else who has been helping us program our subconscious minds: they gave us the furniture which we have kept and which we use in our mental apartment.

Imagine that most of that "furniture" (our negative thinking), because it was hand-me-down furniture, is weary with age. The old tattered sofa is sagging and worn. The chairs are broken and shaky, ready to fall apart if sat in too heavily. The pictures, hanging crookedly on the walls, are yellowed and faint. The kitchen table leans at an angle, the dishes chipped and cracked, no cup has a handle, long since broken away. Coils of bedsprings show through, rusted and bent. The rug on the floor is more patches and holes than it is rug. In these furnishings, a strong new piece of furniture (some positive thought) would seem out of place, but though here and there, there might be a sturdy piece of furniture or two, they are too overrun in the clutter to be noticed at all.

Now let us say that I agree to come over to your home, this mental apartment, and help you get rid of all the old furniture. I tell you that I am going to help you get rid of your old *negative* thinking once and for all. So at four-thirty tomorrow afternoon I arrive and we begin to carry all of your old hand-me-down furniture outside and we store it in the garage. We remove every piece, every dish, every rug, table, bed, sofa, and chair. We take out every old negative self-belief and store it away, safely out of sight.

By six o'clock that evening we have finished, and I leave. After I leave you stand in the middle of your mental apartment. It is empty and spotless. There is not a negative thought, not a sofa, a picture, a book, or a chair in sight. You look around you and think, "This is great! I've gotten rid of all of my old negative thinking. Now I can be a positive thinker!"

That's at six o'clock. You stand around, walk through your mental apartment, and then stand around some more. A little later that evening, after spending an hour or two with nothing but yourself and an empty apartment, what do you suppose you will do? You will go out into the garage, where the old furniture is stored, and get a chair! A little later, you will make another trip to the garage and bring in a table, and maybe a dish or two.

We are most comfortable with the thoughts we have

lived with the most. It makes no difference if those thoughts aren't the best for us—it's what we know, it's what we are most secure in keeping at our side. By nine o'clock you may even have retrieved the trusty old TV. *One by one, you will begin to bring your old trusted and time-worn negative thoughts back into your mental apartment!* Why? Because when I helped you remove the old furniture I didn't give you any *new* furniture to replace it with—I didn't give you any *positive* new thoughts to replace the negative old thoughts.

When you decide to stop thinking negatively, and do not have an immediate, new positive vocabulary to replace the old, you will *always* return to the comfortable, old negative self-talk of the past. If you got rid of your old furniture and stored it in the garage, and you had no new furniture to replace it with, if I were to visit you again in three weeks, you would have all of your old furniture back in your apartment! You would probably have rearranged it, to make it look different, but it would be the same old furniture, the same old programming you had in the first place.

REPLACE THE OLD WITH THE NEW

So instead, let us say that I knock on your door, and I ask you to come outside. There stands a shiny new delivery truck full of the most beautiful furniture you have ever imagined! For the next two or three hours I help you carry all of the beautiful new furniture, your positive new Self-Talk, into your mental apartment. And this time, we don't store the old negative furniture in the garage; we pile it up in a huge pile and set a match to it. We get rid of it. Don't give your old furniture to someone else—*don't pass along your negative self-talk to someone else. After all, that's how you got it in the first place!*

This time when I leave, walk through your mental apartment and look around you. What an incredible sight meets your eyes! What once was a place of tattered hopes and broken-down dreams is now filled with the bright new beginnings of an exciting new you. The new mental furniture stands on the sturdy legs of self-assurance; you have replaced frustration and quiet resignation with the enthusiasm of promise and belief.

That is how positive thinking should work. That is the difference between just believing in positive thinking and actually creating it in your life. It is fine to throw out the old—it is essential. But it is also essential to replace the old with the new—word for word, thought by thought.

The problem has been that in the past, no one gave us the words. No one gave us the word-for-word vocabulary that we needed to replace the negative programming we had learned so well. The right kind of Self-Talk is the key to making all positive thinking work. Without it, for most of us, positive thinking becomes "wishful thinking." And wishful thinking is nothing more than saying to yourself, "I wish I could . . . but I can't." And "I can't" is Level I self-talk—the kind that works against us.

The concept of positive thinking remains an exciting and worthwhile way to think better, live better, and feel better about ourselves. On its own, it will work for a time. Coupled with *the right words,* the special activating, stimulating, directing words of Self-Talk, it can work for a lifetime. If we want to find a method for our minds that helps us reach our goals, we've got to find that method which doesn't just sound good, it has to work—and it has to keep on working. If it doesn't, we fall short of our mark and we wonder why things don't go right for us.

Wanting to be a positive thinker isn't enough. Making the decision to have a positive attitude isn't enough. The human brain says: "Give me more. Give me the words. Give me the directions, the commands, the picture, the schedule, and the results you want. Then I will do it for you. *Give me the words.*"

CHAPTER ELEVEN

The Motivation Myth

THE RADIO TALK show host was saying, "My guest today is a motivational speaker and an author in the field of motivation." He concluded his introduction to the program by turning to me across the microphone and saying, "Shad, are you one of those guys who gets audiences jumping in the aisles and ready to run out and conquer the world?" I think my answer surprised him. My response was, "No, I'm not. In fact, I really don't believe in motivation."

The next few moments may have been the first time there was that much dead silence on his radio show. He had been prepared to talk about the exciting world of motivation and he had just realized that his guest was about to say it doesn't work.

But let me clarify. Some motivation works. It's just that most of it, maybe ninety-five percent of it, doesn't. I recall reading the comment from the training director of a large international corporation. He was interviewed by a national magazine, and the topic was on what is new in training—principally in the field of corporations and large organizations. He said that his company had decided to stop hiring pep-rally motivational speakers. A motivational talk, he had concluded, was much like eating Chinese food for lunch; an hour later you're hungry again. I don't know if that's really true about Chinese food, but it is true about motivation. Most motivation simply doesn't stick. It doesn't stay with you.

There are different kinds of motivation and different kinds of motivators. One of the most popular kinds of motivation consists of an audience of anxious listeners, sitting enthralled while a dynamically enthusiastic speaker weaves for them a web of pure magic, the spun gold of riches and success. For an hour or two he will imbue his listeners with a new sense of destiny, a grand new vision of their unlimited selves, all of them capable of scaling the highest mountains of their imagination, if only they believe that they can.

The members of the audience are given a new lease on life; the only payment required is that they begin the next day as the *new* person, conquering all odds, laying waste their limitations, focusing on the goal and going for it. If you have ever attended a motivational talk such as I am describing, you know that I am being somewhat polite, and kindly understating the magnitude of the mesmerizing that takes place.

Companies and groups of all sizes and descriptions rely on that kind of motivation to pep up their people, give a high point to their conventions and sales meetings, and send the troops away, ready to go out and fight dragons, close more sales, fix problems fast, and reach new heights of achievement.

Large convention center motivational rallies have been held in cities across the United States. These one- or two-day major motivational events have attracted tens of thousands of attendees anxious to spend a day of their lives getting filled up with powerful motivational and inspirational, sure-fire techniques for success, and the clues that will lead to the unlocking of life's greatest rewards.

Popular lecturers and speakers, dynamic orators, enlightening the faithful with the contagious zeal of the greatest Sunday morning sermons, captivate, charm, cajole, and convince their listeners of their ultimate potential. They fascinate, enrapture, entertain, and enchant. They do what they came there to do: *they motivate*.

For the most part, these motivators do a good job. They get people thinking. They paint pictures, a gallery of suggested dreams, which show others what *can* be, what they can do. They are the pied pipers of success, leading the average would-be achiever toward something better. They stimulate minds, inspire new ideas, and reaffirm the resolve to get at it, get something done, accomplish something worthwhile, set some goals, tackle the problems, and move forward. But there is a problem with that kind of motivation: *it is external and it does not last*.

EXTERNAL TEMPORARY MOTIVATION

All *external* motivation is temporary. External motivation is the kind that may wake you up, but it will not keep you awake for long. External motivation is motivation which comes to you from the outside. It may influence you to make a change, but it cannot make the change for you. And it cannot keep you from drifting off course when the motivator is gone. It is the external coach who supports, encourages, demands, and rewards. But when the coach is gone, so is the support, the encouragement, the demand, and the reward.

Let's say that during the summer months you play softball on a local team which has the goal of winning the local tournament. Your team is fortunate to have an exceptional coach. He expects a lot from you but he also gives you a lot of encouragement. He picks you up when you get down, helps you believe that you can win, and lets you know it when you've done a good job. He's a great motivator, and he takes your team all the way to the top. He has been your friend, your ally, and your strongest supporter. You relied on him for your motivation and you got it.

Then the season is over and the coach goes home. What do you suppose he takes with him? Your motivation. *He* was your motivation. Now he is no longer around, and you have to get your motivation from somewhere else. Why? Because that motivation was external. It all came to you from the outside of you. And it was all *temporary* motivation.

All of our external motivation works the same way. Keep giving us the motivation and we will do better. Take it away and we will move, mentally, back to where we were before the motivation began. We may have progressed or grown or achieved something in the process, but we did so with someone else's energy; it was not our own.

That is why so many of the hopeful attendees at so many motivational talks get pumped up, full of energy, ready to conquer the world, and then slow down or stop dead in their tracks weeks, days, or even hours after the speech is over. The inspiration they felt so strongly during the message is no longer there. The energy and enthusiasm which whelmed up inside of them is gone. The motivator left town. And so did most of the dream. All that often remains is enough left over to remind you of what you could have done but didn't do.

That's because the convention hall or the banquet room was filled with individuals who, unless they had first learned how to do it differently, had taken their old computer programs with them. The motivators were talking to a room filled with old computer programs—programs which were designed to subconsciously *reject* the new information which the motivator was trying to feed in! It takes more than an hour or two to override the old programming and replace it with the new.

It takes more than a rousing speech to erase and replace those internal programs which tell us we should know better than to suddenly believe that we are powerful champions of success. Lasting motivation takes more than the single reading of a book, getting an occasional talk from the supervisor or manager, or the encouragement of a friend.

The external motivation tells us that we can do anything we want to accomplish. Our poorly programmed internal motivator, our subconscious mind, says, "Rubbish!" We may believe the external motivator for a time—we *want* to believe it! But our longtime, comfortable old program patiently waits for us to come to our senses, believe what our past programming has taught us, and stop this nonsense about wanting to be a superachiever. Whether or not we are capable of achieving doesn't make a bit of difference to our subconscious minds. They are still acting on the tens of thousands of previous directions which told us "No! . . . you can't."

An hour or two of someone else telling us that "we can do it!" simply doesn't have a chance. The intentions were great. The talk was inspiring. The ideas were incredible. But when the coach goes home—so does the motivation.

How much better it would be if that same inspiring speaker spoke to a crowded hall of *positive Self-Talkers*—people with new disks in their computers, just waiting to get filled up. A subconscious mind which has erased the old negatives and replaced them with new positives is the most fertile ground for growth and achievement we will ever find.

MANAGING OTHERS

Corporate executives and training directors should take note. If you have ever wondered why your own motivational programs must be repeated or reinforced so frequently, it is because in the human brain, it is physiologically impossible for momentary external motivation to create permanent change. You can step up the amount of motivation and training you offer, increase its frequency and never let the coach go home. But if he ever does, the old conditioning that is running your employees' ships will once again take over. Some of the external motivation may last a little longer than others, but all of it will eventually slow down and stop.

If you are responsible in any way for the training, development, motivation, inspiration, or direction of other people, regardless of your field—whether you are a business person, educator, clergyman, parent, or friend—remember that the people you are talking to *want to believe* in the best you are giving them. But always remember that their progress toward accepting, believing in, and acting upon it, is first and always filtered through their own previous conditioning and programming.

If you truly want to reach them, work first with their self-talk. It is the unconscious self-talk they are using today which will determine whether they subconsciously open the door to you—or turn you away. Work first with the self-talk which is guiding them now, share with them the Self-Talk which will open the door, and then watch what happens. People want to improve, change for the better. Help them, with positive Self-Talk, see themselves in a different way, and they will.

Another problem with external motivation, and the problem which we should be most aware of, is that a lot of it works *against* us. Here's how it works: We go to a motivational talk. It's a good talk and we get motivated and inspired. If it is a *great* talk, by the time it is over we will have set some new sights and made an irrevocable commitment to make some important change for the better. We may even have set some specific goals to do just that.

Then we go home. We get back to the details and distractions of everyday life. Our old programming quietly reconvinces us that we are capable of less than that person on the stage was trying to get us to believe. We are not even aware that there is a powerful internal mechanism at work busily beginning to override the new inspiration we got from the speaker. Eventually our internal programming wins out. We had, while we listened to the trainer, readjusted our sights higher and set new goals. But after a few minor defeats, we start to agree once again with our old opinion of ourselves, and we fail to reach the goal.

The disappointment of that failure, large or small, often takes the individual backwards! I know potentially great men and women who got themselves so enthused about their new goals that when they failed to achieve them, gave up completely. I have known people who left their jobs to look elsewhere, disappointed in themselves (though they usually blame someone or something else), convinced that what they were told they could accomplish was a fairy tale or worse.

No one told them that before they could make a sweeping change in their lives they would first have to make one minor change within themselves. No one told them that they could have achieved those exciting goals if they had first learned how to talk to themselves.

There are, of course, many kinds of external motivation which look nothing like a motivational rally or pep talk. In fact, most of the motivation we receive is far less obvious. We rely on friends, books, family, luck, problems, achievements, and social pressures to tell us what to do and to keep us doing it.

One of our greatest daily motivators is the heap of demands of daily living. That is often what gets us up in the morning, gets us going, and motivates us to do most of what we do throughout the day. Most of us will admit that we feel we "have to," "should," "need to" or are "supposed to" do most of what we do. We have even found a popular word to express the result of too much of that kind of motivation: *stress*. But these external motivators are also temporary. The motivation exists until the demands go away.

Since the real meaning of the word motivation is "to

put into motion," it seems to me that when it comes right down to it, if a vote were taken, most of us would rather decide for ourselves what should put us "into motion" than to have someone else decide for us.

THE ONLY MOTIVATION THAT LASTS

How about being your own motivator? How about taking charge and putting yourself back in control? You can, just by learning that all true motivation—the only kind that lasts, the only kind you can count on—is *internal* motivation.

Imagine having a coach that stayed with you, season after season and every day in between. Imagine not needing to wait for someone else to get you charged up and moving. Imagine being able to rely on yourself to always automatically and unconsciously energize your spirit, focus your attention, and keep you in tune, on top, in touch, and going for it! Can you imagine never again needing someone else to prod or push you into activating your own best efforts?

Your own *internal coach* is waiting to do just that. It is your best friend, your closest ally, your strongest believer. It will show you the best in yourself and help you achieve it. It will give you direction, put purpose in your stride, strengthen your will, and give you unquestioned belief. It is loyal to the end. It is the coach that never goes home. It is the ultimate motivator. It will never fail you. It cannot—it is *you!*

CHAPTER TWELVE

Not Hypnosis—Not Subliminal

I AM OFTEN ASKED if Self-Talk is a form of self-hypnosis. In some ways, Self-Talk looks and acts, at first glance, like a form of self-hypnosis, but there is an important difference between the two: hypnosis takes the control of your receptive mind and programs it without the benefit of conscious control—hypnosis is not effected during the normal "waking" state. Self-Talk helps you achieve the same objective *consciously;* it is accomplished each day, as a part of your normal waking state.

Hypnosis requires the subject (you) to enter what is called a "trance" state, one of several levels of consciousness which open doors to the subconscious mind. The verbal suggestions to enter the trance state can be given to you by someone else, or with practice, by yourself, using specially worded tapes, you can enter the trance state on your own. In the field of psychology and in certain areas of medical science, there is still some disagreement about what, exactly, takes place when a person becomes hypnotized.

Most researchers agree that when individuals are

placed in a hypnotic state, they are more receptive to certain kinds of suggestions. There also appears to be less "clutter" between the conscious mind and the unconscious mind—the distractions of the so-called conscious mind are reduced and the individual appears to be more open to subconscious suggestions and directions of various kinds.

Some experienced practitioners in the field of hypnosis have concluded that hypnotic states are natural states of mind. So natural, in fact, that according to them, we are "hypnotically" influenced daily by subtle subconscious suggestions of which we are not even aware.

I have met people and had personal friends who have told me how hypnosis helped them reduce weight, stop smoking, or played an important role in overcoming fears. I have no doubt that for them, it worked. I have observed troubled souls who sought, and found, with the aid of an experienced hypnotherapist, the source of, and ultimately the "cure" for the problems they faced.

While there are medical doctors, psychiatrists, and psychologists who question hypnosis or denounce it as a pseudo-science, there are also other professionals in the same fields who attest to having used hypnosis to help their patients reduce pain, relieve anxiety, control stress, or change habits. They have told us that hypnosis offers us a way to dramatically affect our health, our jobs, and our personal lives.

Their experience has taught us that many of the early fears about hypnosis were unfounded; when hypnotized, whether knowingly or not, we will not suddenly fall prey to the wishes of some mental magician who tricks our minds into obeying his every command.

Hypnosis has not won the overwhelming acceptance of the scientific community. There are, however, within that same community of educated individuals, those who claim that hypnosis is not a fad espoused by the esoteric—a non-chemical, mental wonder drug which will cure all ills. Instead, these individuals view hypnosis as a legitimate tool which should be researched, perfected, accepted and used as a contributing part of our modern-day science.

If you elect to use Self-Talk, and to become a conscious, positive "Self-Talker," it is important that you understand why hypnosis is not a part of Self-Talk—even if hypnosis were to live up to the claims which some of its practitioners ascribe to it.

The reason that Self-Talk does not use hypnosis for its effectiveness has nothing to do with whether hypnosis works or not. The reason has to do with something called *responsibility*—personal responsibility.

TAKING RESPONSIBILITY
FOR YOURSELF

When I was young, I somehow got the impression that "responsibility" was a bad word. A lot of us had similar conditioning. We usually heard the word *responsibility* used in a way that was connected with somebody who was either doing something wrong, or wasn't doing what he was supposed to do: "Who's responsible for this?" was the usual adult question to the child when something got broken.

When a teenager had done something wrong, or wasn't living up to expectations, the typical admonition was, "Why aren't you more responsible?" And those questionable words of motivation were often capped off with, "Can't you take any responsibility for yourself?" Somehow the word *responsible* was never connected to good things; it was always used when things were going wrong.

"Responsibility" means something far beyond that—something much more important! Personal responsibility is at the root of everything we think, do, conceive, fail at, or achieve in our lives. *Personal responsibility is the bedrock of all individual action.* Responsibility does not mean "duty" or "burden." It is not the measure of our liability or our accountability: it is the basis of our individual determination to accept life and to fulfill ourselves within it.

The day you were born, there is a good chance that there were a few other people around helping you into the world. Your mother was there, probably a doctor, and maybe a nurse or two. But no matter who patted you on the backside when you came struggling into human life, you took your first breath alone. No matter what help you may have received, *you* took that first breath by yourself. And the next breath, and the next. *You* did that! You may have had some help along the way, but the breaths you took were your own. No one breathed them for you.

One day, each of us will die. If you have ever stood at the bedside of someone who was passing out of this world, you know that no matter how tightly you might have held that loved one's hand, their last breath was breathed alone. When you or I take our last breath, in earthly matters, we will breathe it alone.

In spite of everything that anyone can do to help, in spite of the doctors and the assistants, in spite of the needs and tears of those who stay behind, when we leave, we will leave alone. There may be abundant spirits to guide us, but of those we leave on earth behind us, not one of them can share that journey with us. We take our first breath by ourselves. And we take our last breath alone.

How then is it that somewhere in between, in that time we call *life,* we expect someone else to do our breathing for us?!

No one will ever breathe one breath for us. No one will ever think one thought that is ours. No one will *ever* stand in our bodies, experience what happens to us, feel our fears, dream our dreams, or cry our tears. We are born, live, and leave this life *entirely* on our own. That "self," and the divine spirit which drives it, are what we have. No one else can ever live a single moment of our lives for us. That we must do for ourselves. *That* is *responsibility.*

Personal responsibility is the essence of *self.* I, for one, would rather not give that up. Why would we *ever* want someone else to do our thinking for us?

The use of hypnosis may be a fine and worthwhile way to set our minds in certain ways. If it can successfully aid in treating pain without chemicals, I applaud it. If it can assist us in other ways, as an adjunct to other methods, I accept its positive results. But given a choice between taking conscious personal responsibility and trance-state solutions, we should opt for those methods which give us personal control—those which demand and utilize the long-term benefits of taking charge—taking personal responsibility. With active, daily Self-Talk, you are consciously in control and in charge of every change you are making within yourself. With hypnosis you are not.

SUBLIMINAL CONDITIONING

There is a near cousin of hypnosis which has become popular in recent years. It is often called "subliminal" learning. The concept of subliminal learning works like this: While you are listening to a cassette of something of an "ordinary" nature, such as soft music, the sound of rain, or a soothing stream in the forest, you are also hearing, unconsciously, messages which have been subliminally hidden within or under the other sounds.

An example of this would be a cassette tape of specially recorded music which also has recorded into the soundtrack an inaudible spoken message. You hear the music, but you do not consciously hear the voice which is speaking to you. It may be convincing you to lose weight, reduce your stress, increase your capabilities, improve your relationship with your loved one, or make more money, depending on the subject that is being covered on the recording.

I have reviewed a variety of cassette tapes which utilize the concept of subliminal learning, in order to assess their effectiveness. I have studied what appear to be objective case studies of the use of subliminal learning to effect a change in human behavior. Does this kind of subliminal programming work? And if it does, is it the result of the actual subliminal message or does it help because we *think* it is working—a kind of subliminal placebo?

Most of us remember the stories from the nineteen-fifties and the early sixties when it was reported that movie theaters were inserting short subliminal mes-

sages into the film to get us to rush out to the refresh-
ment stand and buy a soft drink and some popcorn.
The government got interested, theaters were cau-
tioned to stop using subliminal advertising messages in
their films, and the furor over "mind control" died
down and was, for the most part, forgotten.

There remain, however, a number of elusive stories
about certain shopping malls that word a subliminally
recorded message into their background music at
Christmas time in order to reduce shoplifting. I have
also observed, by viewing recent high-action movies
on video tape, frame-by-frame stills of skulls and other
horrifying pictures, carefully edited into action se-
quences of the film. I have no doubt whatsoever that,
when viewed at regular speed, "subliminally," unconsciously, these split-second images create the desired
effect in our minds. Subliminal intrusions on our unconscious minds do affect us.

Can the same techniques be used to convince us to
use a certain brand of perfume or buy a new line of
cosmetics? I think that most advertising agency executives would privately vouch for the fact that they do. If
the same subliminal techniques work, could they be
used to influence our vote in an election? If the human
mind is, as some have said, the playground of the
powerful, those who would manipulate and control our
thoughts must certainly be having a field day!

By not taking responsibility for our own thoughts,
we leave our minds open to the whims of others. As
individuals, we deserve better—we are capable of
exerting more control over ourselves, our own minds,
individually, than any outside control or influence
which anyone else could possibly have over us.

Subliminal learning techniques may one day prove
to be safe and solid bastions of the edifice of scientific

learning. But they require you to trust completely those who are silently feeding information to your mind. I would still encourage you to vote your own vote, think for yourself, be *aware* of what you are programming into your own subconscious mind.

There are those who will say that hypnosis has its place. I believe that it does. There are those who will say that "subliminal" mind techniques are effective. They may be right. But I encourage you to take the responsibility for *you* and everything you accept and do as a part of your own given birthright! You deserve the right to own and control your own thoughts! *You are your thoughts.* Don't ever let anyone else have dominion over them.

THINK FOR YOURSELF

If you use self-hypnosis as a tool for your own growth, and it has worked for you in the past, and if you choose to use Self-Talk as a part of that tool, the combination of your own self-hypnosis and your new Self-Talk should work for you as well. If your meditation or your mantra of self-direction includes the words of Self-Talk, then your meditation, and you, will benefit from them. But always remember that some of the greatest minds, some of the greatest achievers which this earth has ever known, achieved their greatness with only three overriding attributes: spirit, conviction, and hard work.

When you learn to talk to yourself in the right way, you do not need the conviction of a hypnotic trance to give you the inner strength that you desire; you do not need to wait, hopefully, for some subliminal message to convince you.

Your own Self-Talk to your own inner self is, and always will be, your surest form of inner defense and inner strength. Combine that with your personal source of spiritual strength—and no one, *nothing* can override it. Use it! Employ the resources of your own mind. Call them to action! Think for yourself. Speak for yourself. Educate and program your own mind in the manner of your own choosing. No one else should do that for you. No one else has the right.

CHAPTER THIRTEEN

If It Isn't Simple, It Won't Work

THE MORE WE have learned about Self-Talk, the more ways we have found to use it—ways that make it easier to practice and learn and make it more lasting and effective at the same time. No idea, no matter how good, will work if it doesn't get used. When I studied the field of self-help and examined the many concepts available, I found some self-help concepts that made a lot of sense and could have worked, but they were too difficult to put into practice.

Even with the most ardent self-improvement enthusiasts, any "program" that takes too much time, requires too much sacrifice, or is too complex to use easily, will not get used. I suspect that some of the best self-improvement books and cassette programs ever written are gathering dust on a shelf or are tucked away in some closet, safely out of sight and out of mind behind a stack of two-year-old magazines, which will also not get read.

Self-help books and tapes too often fall into the same category as home-exercise machines that were used once and put away. They are like the barbells and gym sets, sand-filled weight-loss belts, jogging shoes and home-study foreign language courses—all of which seemed like a good idea at the time we bought them, but they took too much work. So we hid them away and told ourselves that we would bring them back out of hiding and get started using them a little later. Instead of having a revered place in the family den, and eventually being worn out through overuse, the books, gadgets, and costly gizmos of self-improvement often end up on the bargain tables of neighborhood garage sales.

I have met dozens of people who have told me about the self-help books and programs they have started, but have never even finished—let alone put into practice. I can sympathize with them. Wading through a self-help program which demands a monastic regimen of diligence and self-sacrifice does not stimulate enthusiastic involvement. And even the simplest of programs are hard enough to stick with.

PUTTING IT OFF

When it comes to spending our time doing those things which could do the most for us in return, self-improvement rarely comes first. The normal distractions of everyday living are enough to keep even the most hopeful and needing individual from expending the time or the energy to make a break and get ahead. Self-improvement is one of those strange remedies which, though the advantages it offers should put it first on our list, we all too easily put off doing anything about it when we need it most, postponing our decision to fix the leaking roof until a day when there is no more rain in sight. We know we need it, but other things come first.

When I first witnessed the sometimes astonishing effects that people were experiencing in their lives after putting into practice some of the self-help ideas and techniques which they had learned, I was dismayed when I saw so many others failing to do the same things. I was saddened to see the results which low self-esteem and negative self-belief were creating in so many lives, when it was apparent that with a little effort on anyone's part, it did not have to be that way.

But I also observed how few people who wanted to make a significant change in their lives had the determination and self-motivation to *work* at making the change. It was only later, after I had analyzed the "methods" people were using to make the changes, that I understood why so few were using them. Unless an individual's predisposition to self-determination was strong enough—unless a person's heredity and early conditioning created an attitude and a will which *demanded* improvement and change—the normal obstacles of day-to-day life stopped them short.

Most of us know we could do better. I doubt that I could find ten people who, when pressed, would not say that they, too, would like to improve *something* about themselves. We are also aware of the benefits which creating improvements in ourselves creates in our lives.

We are well aware of the material advantages we would like to have—a new home or car, new clothes, furniture, more money in the bank, and anything we have set our hearts on that a little extra money could give us. Most of us would also like to have more time, more freedom to do the things we want—time to travel, time to spend with our families, time to relax, time to enjoy, time to create, or time to spend with others doing the things we most like to do. And many of us would like to improve our education, learn something new, take up new interests, and develop our skills.

THE COMPETITION OF DAILY LIVING

Through some natural law of cause and effect, when we improve ourselves, the things we would like to have in our lives follow naturally. Improve *who* you are, and by that same law, you will improve your life. The more successful you become *inside,* the more successes you will automatically create on the outside. But making changes on the inside is seldom as easily accomplished as we would like it to be. When we decide to change, we are suddenly confronted with a wall of obstacles we would rather not have bargained for. When we commit to change, we suddenly find ourselves confronted with some unexpected competition.

When we want to improve ourselves in some way, we are not just competing with our old programming; we are competing with the requirements of daily living. Each of us has three "resources" which allow us to get through any given day. Those resources are our *time,* our *energy,* and our *minds* (what and how we think).

Our desire to improve ourselves competes with the time we spend working, taking care of our families, and taking care of the rest of our needs. It competes with the energy we consume doing everything necessary just to keep our lives in some reasonable order. Sometimes, most days for some of us, there is just no energy left. Our desire to improve ourselves competes with the demands which we or others have placed on us mentally, as well. We have so many things to think about, so many small and big decisions to make, things to figure out, problems to solve, things to consider, understand, and deal with.

We are so busy taking care of first things first that we have no time, energy, or thought left to take care of the one thing that could make all of the other things work better. We are too busy fixing the train to realize that we are on the wrong track. We are too busy staying alive to figure out how to *live*.

I remember the excitement I first felt when, many years ago, I happened upon what I thought to be the most exceptional self-improvement idea I had ever encountered. It was a simple idea which would require only that I spend twenty minutes each night writing my goals, reviewing my progress, and mentally visualizing reaching each goal I was setting. I didn't have to be convinced that if I spent even that small amount of time each day concentrating on my goals, especially at night just before I went to sleep dreaming about them, that I could achieve anything I wanted. It is an old idea—and it works.

What I did not know then, but soon learned, was that even twenty minutes a night is sometimes hard to come by. When you are holding down a job, raising a family, and going back to school with a full-time college-level course load, just trying to get five or six hours of sleep a night is a challenge. When my mind was somewhere between studying for a psychology exam and finishing a business plan that was due at eight o'clock at the office the next morning, the twenty minutes I was supposed to spend each night working out my goal plan and "improving myself" soon moved from an exalted position of importance to an impossible chore. It's hard to study your goals when you can't keep your eyes open.

My first experience with self-improvement was not unique. The idea was great—and still is. But, as I was to learn later, the practical application of that great idea was not practical.

THE RIGHT TOOLS

To this day, millions of people have tried the same kinds of marvelous ideas, with the same results. Of those, I doubt that more than a few thousand stuck it out and stayed with it. I applaud those who have. But I feel deeply for those who could not. Those who wanted to achieve but did not, or could not, had somewhere inside themselves, wanted to achieve just as much as those who did. They just didn't have the right tools. They didn't find a way to improve themselves that would work for them. Maybe they weren't as dedicated as the few who did succeed. Maybe the other commitments in their lives got in the way. But they wanted to achieve, and if they had found the right way to do it, they would have.

How, then, can any good and true idea which clearly could improve our lot in life, hope to succeed when few of us have the time, physical energy, or mental energy left over even to give it a try? The answer to that question is very important. It is the answer which will make one good idea work when another will not: *For any self-improvement concept to be successful, it has to be simple. It has to be easy to use. And when put into practice, it has to work!*

CHAPTER FOURTEEN

The New Techniques

THE TECHNIQUES THAT make Self-Talk work so well are simple and they are surprisingly easy to use. Some of the techniques require spending time using them, but some of the techniques require no time at all. There are five different methods for using Self-Talk; you may choose to use some or all of them:

SILENT SELF-TALK

This is the Self-Talk that goes on all of the time, although we are usually not aware of it. Silent Self-Talk can be either a conscious or an unconscious internal dialogue. When you begin to replace old self-talk with positive new Self-Talk, this is one of the easiest and most natural techniques to use. Even now, after just becoming aware of the difference between the negative self-talk of Level I and Level II, there is a good chance that you are already starting to use the positive Self-Talk of Level III and Level IV when you silently talk to yourself. It is an easy change to make. It takes more awareness than effort, and soon becomes a natural and automatic Self-Talk habit.

Silent Self-Talk includes anything and everything you think about yourself or anything else around you. It is that subtle shift in your attitude from ever again looking at things in a negative way to looking at everything in a more positive, productive way.

Instead of waking up in the morning and telling yourself you wish you didn't have to get out of bed, your new Self-Talk should tell you that it's a great day to be alive—and it's time to get at it. Since most of those things we call problems are really only *perceived* as problems, the way you look at each of them determines whether they really are or not; you need only tell yourself to see them in a better way. If you think that might sound a little too easy, try it for a day and see what happens.

Remember, when you begin rephrasing your self-talk from the old to the new, your old programming will try to talk you out of it. So when you get started, start first with the decision to not listen to the earlier negative program which tries to tell you that it won't work. Remember, too, that your old self-talk is a habit. It feels natural and it feels comfortable even if it is negative. By knowing what to expect, you will be ready to meet that old self-talk head on, override it, and begin building a new habit.

Within even a day or two, you will start to notice everything you have been saying to yourself that could work against you. When you have made the decision to throw the old furniture out of your mental apartment, you'll know when you are trying to bring it back in. Put your foot down. Get tough! Keep it out.

As you get started, during each day, listen to everything you say when you talk to yourself. Make a mental note of anything you think or say to yourself that sounds like the wrong kind of self-talk and immediately turn it around and rephrase it in the positive. "I just can't seem to get organized today" immediately becomes "I am organized and in control, today especially!" When you hear yourself say something like "I've really got a problem with this . . ." turn it around and say "I can handle this! I'm a capable person and I handle problems well." "I just can't seem to lose weight" becomes "Losing weight is never a problem for me. I eat exactly what I should and only the right, healthy amount—I'm losing weight and looking great!"

Instead of telling yourself that you're tired—at a time of the day when you can't afford to be tired—*immediately* tell yourself that you have plenty of energy and enthusiasm. And if it doesn't suddenly make you jump up and down with energy, that's okay; you're working on a whole new way to talk to yourself and you are starting to give your subconscious mind a new set of directions. Just keep doing it every chance you get and it will start to work for you. How we "feel"—tired or energetic, listless or enthusiastic—is mental and *chemical;* it is physiological.

Think of a time when you feel like you don't want to even get up out of the chair. It has been a long day, you worked hard, and you are physically and mentally exhausted. Then the phone rings and it is just the right phone call at just the right moment, someone calling with good news, or someone who is the most important person in the world to you. What suddenly happens to your energy? What happens to your enthusiasm? A surge of adrenaline hits your system and brings you back to life *instantly*. Has anything really changed? Just the signals you sent to your brain, and, in turn, the switches your brain turned on for you, sending messages to every part of your system telling you to suddenly feel great when only moments before you couldn't get out of the chair.

Many of the messages you give yourself through your silent self-talk may not be as obvious. But the brain responds just as immediately and produces results, whether they are noticed or not, that are just as powerful. Remember, the thoughts you think are electrical impulses which direct the brain to turn important switches in your mental control center on or off. By replacing your earlier negative or neutral self-talk with new commands, you are activating healthy, productive chemical and electrical control centers in your brain which will automatically work for you instead of against you.

We have all experienced times when one argument in the morning can ruin the whole day. Change the programming. Rephrase your silent thoughts to yourself. Instead of losing a day to depression or dejection, you will gain one more precious day of worthwhile accomplishment. You will feel better emotionally, you will be healthier, both mentally and physically, you will get along better with others. Instead of chalking the day up as a loss, you will have earned yourself another win.

SELF-SPEAK

Anything you say out loud to yourself, or to someone else about yourself, or about anything else, is part of your self-talk. What you say when you are speaking makes up an important part of the pictures and directions you are feeding to your subconscious mind.

It makes sense that if what you say when you are speaking paints the wrong pictures or delivers commands which give yourself counterproductive information, the end result will be that your brain will act on the information in a way that could work against you in any number of ways. Telling a friend that you don't like your job cannot possibly help your job. You may make yourself feel better by getting it off your chest, and in most forms of therapy, that technique is used with some success. But how much better it would be if you were to change your attitude by changing the programming you were giving yourself, especially in those circumstances when the job (or any situation) isn't going to change just by complaining about it.

Your Self-Talk is at the heart of something we call "acceptance." There are times in life when all of us feel compelled to put up with a bad situation. But it is completely up to you whether you let that situation work against you, or make a mental decision to see it in a different way. Your self-speak and other forms of Self-Talk are the determining factors in whether the real you, the inside you, wins or loses.

We make hundreds of comments or statements in any given day. It might not seem all that important to phrase each of the many things you say each day in some positive way. But consider that each of those statements is a directive to your subconscious mind. Then add up those comments and statements over a week, a month, or a year. They add up to tens of thousands of minor but very important subconscious self-directives. They're important all right—they have a whole lot to do with what you accomplish, how you feel, and *who you become*.

The easiest way to determine which of the people around you are the real winners at life and which are not, is to listen to their self-speak—what they say when they talk about anything. Winners use self-speak to build an attitude that produces winning results. It doesn't mean that "winners" don't have problems. It doesn't mean that every day for them is a perfect day. But look at their average scores in winning at life over a few months or a few years. The better their self-speak, the better their score. The more positive their approach, the more successful the results. In time, positive self-speak becomes as much an automatic habit as walking, moving, eating, or sleeping. And when positive self-speak becomes a habit, so do the successes which the self-speak creates.

Listen to everything you say when you speak. Do your words paint the picture for your own subconscious mind you want it to be hearing? If not, change the words. Rephrase them. Learning to build the best in yourself—by learning to give yourself a refreshing new program of self-speak—is one of the greatest gifts you will ever give to yourself. Once mastered, it is a treasure you will never lose.

SELF-CONVERSATION

This form of Self-Talk is one of the easiest to use, and it can also be a lot of fun. Self-conversation is the technique of actually talking to yourself *out loud* and holding down both ends of the conversation all by yourself! Self-conversation is one of the most effective forms of Self-Talk because it engages more of your senses and puts more of you to work programming yourself in the new way. When you have a self-conversation, more of *you* gets involved!

When you first begin to practice conversational Self-Talk, you may want to go into the bathroom and lock the door. When you start talking to yourself out loud, carrying on a conversation with yourself, asking yourself questions and answering them, even your most trusting family members may think you have finally gone over the edge. On one occasion I was flying from Chicago to San Francisco with a layover in Denver on the night of December twenty-third, the night before Christmas Eve. Because of bad weather, our departure from Denver was delayed, and at twenty minutes after eleven at night, we were informed that because of the snowstorm, we would have to spend several hours, or possibly all night, in the Denver airport.

Since it was the busy holiday season, all the planes were packed, and due to the planes being off-loaded at the Denver airport, the lobby and terminal buildings were rapidly filling up with passengers—none of whom were too happy about having to spend the night in the Denver airport, missing their connecting flights, and quite possibly not being able to make it home in time for Christmas Eve. I don't think I've ever seen so many irate people in one place at one time. I thought some of them were going to put their cigars out on the ticket agents' foreheads! Obviously they must have thought the snowstorm was the airline's fault—after all, who would blame God for making it snow the night before Christmas Eve?

After sizing up the situation, I decided this might be a good time for me to practice a little conversational Self-Talk. I wanted to get home just as much as anyone else, and I thought this would be a good time to test the effect of some instant programming. I looked around and noticed that the seats in the waiting area were filling up fast, and I noticed three seats side-by-side in a row were still vacant. So I walked over, sat down in the middle of the three seats, and proceeded to talk to myself—out loud.

In a clear, confident and loud voice I turned to myself and said, "Hi, Shad! Looks like we're grounded!" "Yup!" I answered, just as confidently, "What would you like to do?" "Let's talk!"

And thus began one of the most interesting conversations I believe I have ever had—*with myself! It worked!* Not only was my stress level lower than anyone else's in that airport, but no one else sat down on either side of me all night!

There is, however, a less conspicuous and safer way to use self-conversation, and it is a way I recommend you try at your next available opportunity. I refer to it as "shower talk" and it works like this: Tomorrow morning, when you step into the shower, say "Good morning!" to yourself. Say it out loud, and say it with a smile in your voice. Greet the day with your chin up, your attitude high, and tell yourself just how great the day ahead is going to be. "You look *great* today! You feel good, you're in good shape, and you're ready to tackle anything!" And then respond—give yourself an answer back. "I feel *terrific!* Today especially! I feel good, I like who I am and I'm glad to be alive and going for it!"

Even two or three minutes of that kind of rousing *internal* motivation can get you started on the right foot, facing the day, looking forward to it, and get you moving and believing in a way that can change an average day into an exceptional day. And it *works!* Think how much better that kind of invigorating, positive day-starting, confidence-building self-dialogue can be than the other ways we often use to start our day.

When I am doing a training program for a corporation or for an organization, when I talk about getting yourself started in the morning with that kind of Self-Talk—self-*conversation*—of the most activating and vitalizing kind, I usually see in the audience in front of me, a few faces which are registering what looks like something between amusement and incredulity. I must be kidding! But a few weeks later, after they have had a chance to try it a while for themselves, I hear a different story. They try it and it works.

Why *not* start your day out with the absolute best about yourself? Why not come alive, *tell* yourself what you *can* do that day instead of groggily shaking your head over what you *cannot?* It has worked for business managers, salespeople, office workers, construction workers, athletes, students—anyone who wants to make today, tomorrow, and every day *count*.

Although you can carry on a self-conversation silently, you will find that when you talk to yourself out loud you are forcing yourself to put your thoughts into words. That helps you clarify your thinking on the subject and become much more specific than you are when you're just letting thoughts drift through your mind.

One of the benefits of talking to yourself in this way, out loud, and carrying on a conversation with yourself is that this allows you to ask yourself questions and get straightforward answers. When you first try this you might be surprised at the answers you get. We know ourselves pretty well—better than we sometimes think we do. The result is that most of the answers we get when we ask ourselves the right questions are the *real* answers—answers that get us to stop kidding ourselves and get down to the facts.

When you first begin to talk out loud to yourself you might feel a little foolish. I know I did. But in a day or two the benefits will outweigh the minor embarrassment it might have taken to get started. In a short while, you will find yourself talking to yourself in the car, while you are alone in the office, while you're on a walk—anywhere at all.

Use a few of those precious moments of privacy we cherish so much. Tell yourself that you're okay—that you are *better* than okay! Go ahead, say it out loud! If you have a question you haven't found the answer to, ask it. *Take counsel with yourself.* You've got a pretty good friend in there who has been waiting to hear from you.

SELF-WRITE

Some people have told me that writing their own Self-Talk has been one of the most enjoyable projects they have ever embarked upon for themselves.

Other, equally motivated, would-be self-talkers have told me that *using* Self-Talk, reading Self-Talk, or listening to Self-Talk was great, but they simply couldn't find the time or perhaps the creativity within themselves to write, phrase for phrase, the Self-Talk they needed to achieve the changes they wanted to make.

Self-*write* is the kind of Self-Talk that you write out, word for word, for yourself. It is Self-Talk that is phrased in specific Self-Talk statements which deal directly with the most important new instructions you want to deliver to your subconscious mind—the new programming you want to work on most. (In Chapter Twenty-Two you will learn the specific steps to follow to write your own Self-Talk.)

When I first explored finding practical ways to put Self-Talk to work, I began by writing out Self-Talk for each area of personal self-improvement and then establishing a daily routine of reading the Self-Talk to myself. It was effective but it took time and diligence. Other individuals who tried this method met with the same results, but in each case, the effectiveness was directly relative to the effort that the self-talker was willing to put into the project.

This early form of Self-Talk was written out on index cards—one Self-Talk statement per card. Eventually, the persistent Self-Talk user would develop a card deck of Self-Talk phrases covering a variety of situations. Anytime a specific goal or problem came up, Self-Talk phrases from the card deck could be pulled out and used each day until the goal was accomplished or the problem was under control.

Although the results were apparent, the effort it took to create the Self-Talk card deck often got in the way of successfully maintaining an ongoing do-it-your-self Self-Talk program. Eventually, after observing others who used this technique, I came to the conclusion that most people simply are not conditioned to write Self-Talk. The result is that they don't.

To remedy this I wrote examples of specific Self-Talk phrases which covered some forty areas of self-improvement—in all, several hundred individual Self-Talk phrases which others could follow and use to more easily write their own Self-Talk. I was well aware of the fact that a lot of people would rather do just about anything than have to sit down and write—especially something as detailed and precise as the specific wording and phrasing which is required to create the kind of Self-Talk that will reprogram the subconscious mind in just the right way.

That is not to say that writing Self-Talk has to be a chore. But unless you enjoy working with words and are willing to follow the "rules" of wording that work most effectively, no matter how much you wanted to begin using Self-Talk, you could get stopped almost as soon as you got started.

But for those who have learned what to write and how to state it, self-write is an exceptionally effective way to reprogram. It focuses your attention, makes you think, and gets you actively involved in the process of erasing the old negative programming and actively participating in the process of replacing the old with the new. That kind of focus—that amount of *involvement*—fine-tunes your initiative and adds energy to your determination.

By writing out your own Self-Talk, you increase your awareness of your objectives—it gets you more *interested,* and interest creates *energy*. The more energy you put into anything, the better the chance it will work for you. I stated earlier that when it comes to finding a way to improve yourself, if it isn't simple, it won't work. So before you decide whether or not writing your own Self-Talk will be simple and easy for you, you should try it for yourself. If it doesn't work for you, there are other means to the end. If self-write *does* work for you, then you will not only enjoy the process—you will be delighted with the results.

TAPE-TALK

The emergence of Self-Talk on tapes came about almost more by accident than by design. Several years ago, during the time I was writing my encyclopedic compilation of Self-Talk for every possible situation, I wanted to lose some weight.

At the time, when I wanted to use some new Self-Talk for myself, I would carefully write out the Self-Talk phrases on individual index cards and post them around my mirror where I could read them out loud or silently to myself while I got ready for work in the morning. I found that reading Self-Talk each morning was a great way to start the day. It got me moving in the right direction and in the right frame of mind to tackle the day ahead.

Before trying Self-Talk to help me lose the weight I wanted to lose, I had tried just about everything else—diets that didn't work, weight-loss clinics that I didn't keep going to, self-created diet programs (usually called starving yourself), and combination programs which consisted of things like exercising for thirty minutes and then drinking nothing but grapefruit juice.

Somehow it always seemed that the more I exercised the hungrier I got, and the more weight I took off the more I felt I should reward myself with "a little something extra"—which usually amounted to something I shouldn't eat because it would put more pounds back on than the pounds I had just taken off. My story was just like the stories of tens of thousands of other weight-conscious dieters who took it off and put it right back on.

But what if, I asked myself, I wrote a special set of Self-Talk cards for losing weight—and keeping it off? After all, Self-Talk was already working for me and for thousands of other people in other important areas of our lives; why not put Self-Talk to the ultimate test?

I began by writing out my Self-Talk for weight loss on my morning-reading index cards and taped them to the mirror. I wrote the very best about myself—my weight, how I ate, my health, my energy—everything I knew would paint a brand-new picture of myself for my subconscious mind. I created the Self-Talk that would create a healthier, thinner "me," with every word of it phrased and stated in just the right way.

I wrote dozens of Self-Talk cards, each of them telling me the best about myself, each of them completing another piece of the picture of me that I most wanted to become.

I had learned much earlier that when you want to fix a problem or achieve a goal, you have to fix more than the symptoms—you have to give yourself a complete diet of Self-Talk covering every facet and every phase of your life which created the problem, or every area of your thinking which was tying you to the old mental programs. So I wrote Self-Talk on self-esteem, Self-Talk for self-confidence, will power, and determination. I wrote Self-Talk which kept my spirits up so I would stay with it, and Self-Talk that talked to me about feeling good, having more energy, and Self-Talk that would keep me from using food to solve some other problem I hadn't worked on yet.

When you want to use Self-Talk to effect a change in your life, it does *not* work to fix only the symptom. So I wrote Self-Talk that got behind the symptoms and into the causes, Self-Talk that would put me back in control, pep me up, and keep me at it.

Each morning I read the cards, one by one, and I began to notice their effect. They were starting to work. Slowly but surely I was beginning to believe what the cards were telling me. But just as surely, I noticed that putting myself through a morning regimen of reading my Self-Talk cards was becoming difficult to stay with.

We all know how some mornings can be. There are other things to think about. Sometimes we simply don't have the time to spend time improving ourselves. Mornings can be a hassle, and spending an extra ten to fifteen minutes each morning soon proved to be an encumbrance on my schedule and my family's schedule. During that time, I think some of the weight I was starting to lose I lost just because I didn't get to breakfast before it was time to leave for the office.

AN EVEN BETTER WAY

There had to be a better way! I knew how well Self-Talk worked. I had watched it work for me and I had witnessed its results in others. But I knew that there had to be an easier way.

Several years prior to that time, in 1968, I had developed early versions of self-improvement tape programs for a sales company. I had written and produced one cassette program in particular which consisted mostly of an early, somewhat primitive form of "I can do it!" Self-Talk for a company which wanted a motivational pep-talk cassette tape which their salespeople could listen to when their sales were down. At that same time I had also written an early version Self-Talk tape for myself which I had used to help me reach some of the professional and financial goals I had set for myself.

I suppose if I listened to those original cassette tapes now, I would be a little embarrassed about their distinctly *non*professional quality. But I recalled that they had met with some success, and not only had a few of the salespeople profited by listening to them, but I too had profited just by listening now and then to some reassuring words of encouragement from rather inexpertly written and recorded home-brew cassette tapes.

Later, as each morning I diligently worked at reading the Self-Talk for weight-loss index cards which were posted on my mirror, I began to think about those old tapes. What if I were to take my Self-Talk index cards, stack them up, get a small cassette recorder, and read them one by one, phrase by phrase, onto a cassette tape? Wouldn't that help me overcome the problem of having to read and reread each card each morning? If I put the same Self-Talk on a cassette tape, I reasoned, all I would have to do each morning is pop my weight-loss cassette into the tape player and let it play away!

So that's what I did. I made a tape on eating, a tape on self-esteem, and a tape on physical fitness. I took the Self-Talk that I had been reading each morning from the cards and recorded every word onto the tapes. While I was at it, I decided to tackle some Self-Talk on getting organized, upping my activity, and taking responsibility for myself. Each morning while I was shaving I listened to my cassette tapes. Each day, while I drove to and from my office, and each night, just before I went to sleep, I listened to my new tapes.

In ten and one-half weeks I lost fifty-eight pounds *shaving* and listening to my cassettes! My doctor was amazed. I had made sure when I started my new "program" that I was doing the right things physically—the right food, the right nutrition. I remember getting a call from my doctor's receptionist after I had weighed in at fifty-eight pounds less. She wanted to know what diet I had used!

But what was even more interesting to me was that during the ten and a half weeks I had been losing the weight, my wife, who was putting on her makeup at the other end of the same mirror, had lost twenty-five pounds *eavesdropping on my cassette tapes!*

It was perhaps then, more than at any other time, that I recognized the incredible capability of the subconscious mind, and the natural capability of something as simple as a cassette recorder to help get the job done.

It wasn't long before friends and clients of mine began to ask me to record a Self-Talk tape or two for them. When I did, they began to relate to me the same kinds of results that I had experienced myself and was starting to hear from others. Suddenly there was a method—a *technology* that combined solid self-programming principles with a tool that anyone could use, and yet would work as well as or better than any of the other techniques I had found. In addition, it was a technological tool which functioned in a way which proved to be directly and naturally compatible with the way the brain worked.

Since I first began to recommend that people use cassette tapes as a programming tool for the subconscious, I have received responses from the users, which surprised even me. I *knew* it worked! But by receiving letters and repeatedly hearing the same kinds of results from others, I became resolutely convinced.

WHETHER BELIEVING OR NOT

A typical example is that of a letter I received from a woman who had attended a seminar on Self-Talk and decided to listen to Self-Talk tapes to help her with her "family relationships"—in particular, her relationship with her husband. Things hadn't been going too well for them, financially or otherwise, and she wanted to put things straight. Meanwhile, her husband was showing all the signs of making a slow but predictable departure from the relationship.

The woman had graduated from writing out Self-Talk cards and reading them to herself, to listening to Self-Talk cassettes. She listened to a cassette on improving personal relationships, a tape on self-esteem, a tape on goal-setting, and another tape on taking responsibility for yourself. She listened to her tapes each morning, when she could during the day, and each night just before she went to sleep. To listen to her tapes, the woman used a small, inexpensive portable tape recorder which she purchased at a local discount store. She let the tapes play aloud—not trying to interrupt her husband's television viewing or bother him in the morning—she just played the tapes. According to her, when she first began playing the positive Self-Talk in the background, her husband could not have cared less.

But after a week or two, her husband took her to dinner one evening and during dinner they discussed her tapes. He still showed every sign of disinterest the next day, but as she had learned in the seminar program, "Don't worry too much about what the other people around you think about your Self-Talk. Just keep doing it."

By the end of the third week her husband asked her to replay one of the tapes she had been playing while they were getting dressed one morning. Earlier she had noticed that they were arguing less, but until that morning he had never shown any active interest in the tapes she was listening to each day. Shortly thereafter, the husband began to exhibit noticeable changes in his behavior toward her and toward his attitude about the problems he had been having on his job.

The end result was that *both* of them began to talk more, started making some new plans, and started working together again. *Her* Self-Talk had the same effect on him as it did on her! It made no difference whether he believed in the Self-Talk or not—*his subconscious mind didn't care!*—it simply acted on the new information he was unconsciously programming in. He was, without even thinking about it, accepting the new, more positive programming which was being played as a *background* to their daily lives. Initially, one "believed" and the other did not. It didn't make any difference.

Along with the other great inventions of mankind, the wheel, the printing press, motorized transportation, radio, television, and the computer, I would add the audio cassette tape. Never before in the history of the human race have we had a device which could, when used in the right way, literally *change* our own internal direction as rapidly, as effectively, and as effortlessly as can the audio cassette. Far beyond its common use as a means of playing music or delivering spoken-word discourses on self-improvement, a cassette tape, that simple little plastic shell with its miniature hub of magnetic recording tape, can for the first time, give each of us a way to hear the very best about ourselves anytime and anywhere we choose to put a tape in a cassette player, push a button, and listen to it.

Tape-Talk—Self-Talk on tape—is without a doubt one of the more practical tools for the betterment of mankind, for the betterment of *each of us* individually, than any other self-development tool I have ever encountered.

In your own personal growth, in your own personal program of Self-Talk, it is not essential that you listen to cassettes to reach your goals. You can reach them without having a single cassette player in your home. A little later, however, I am going to show you how to make your own tapes. To do so will take a minimum of effort and you will receive, in return, an unusually effective result.

Tape-talk has some advantages going for it which are as yet unrivaled in the self-development field. The first and most important advantage is that you can listen to tapes *about you* while you are doing something else. You don't have to really listen. Your subconscious mind will be busily programming in the positive new information about you whether you are consciously thinking about it or not. Another advantage in using tapes is that they are convenient—so we use them. If all we have to do is to put a tape in and play it, we soon learn that that is a lot easier than writing out scripts of self-belief, reading and rereading a book, or trying to study a course in self-achievement.

Another important advantage is that tapes, because they are readily available anytime we want to use them, become a coach which uses the right Self-Talk to give us immediate external motivation while it programs our subconscious minds with a winning script of *internal* motivation.

One of my favorite Self-Talk tapes is entitled, "Believing in Incredible You." It is impossible to listen to that tape without feeling better, thinking better, *doing* better, from the first few minutes the tape starts to play. And while it is gearing me up and getting me going, filling me up with the kind of enthusiasm that turns an average day into an exceptional day, it is also carefully and busily reprogramming me to make *every* day more effective, more productive, more self-fulfilling in every way. That kind of tape is like having a personal coach, a best friend, standing at your side, encouraging, motivating, uplifting, believing, and pushing you forward *that day*, helping you extract and achieve the best from yourself.

If you do not choose to record your own, you may choose to listen to specially recorded Self-Talk tapes which are commercially available. But either way, if you would like to avail yourself of one of the most worthwhile methods of recreating your own future to the good, I encourage you to listen to Self-Talk on tape. Of all the ways to talk to yourself—positively—cassettes are the easiest and most enduring. Just put a Self-Talk tape in the player, push a button, and let it play. Your subconscious mind will be listening—whether you are or not.

* * *

The Self-Talk techniques I have just given you are the most obvious, and simplest and easiest to begin using immediately. But you should know that from the moment you start, whatever "system" you use, any kind of Self-Talk you begin with will be only a beginning. Once any kind of Self-Talk technique starts to work for you, the others almost automatically fall into place, waiting for you to give them a try.

You may decide to try just one of the techniques to see if it will work for you. Use the technique which you feel the most comfortable with first and try it. Then if you want to try something more, go ahead. For now, even if you do nothing more than begin by using silent Self-Talk to just get started, that's fine. There is a phrase of Self-Talk that I have always found especially encouraging and especially true. It reads:

"You're doing pretty good already. And you're just now getting started!"

CHAPTER FIFTEEN

Whatever Your Need or Position in Life

WHEN YOU BEGIN to actively use Self-Talk for yourself, what you use it for first will depend on what you want to fix first or achieve first. But since Self-Talk becomes a self-generating habit—*the more you use it, the more you use it*—its success will depend more on getting started than on what you decide to use it for first.

It makes no difference what you do for a living, what your educational background is, what your problems may be or what your goals are. It doesn't matter whether you have succeeded or failed in the past; Self-Talk works the same for everyone. *The workings of the human brain are completely indifferent to your station in life*. Anyone can use Self-Talk and benefit from its results.

To give you an example of the many ways in which the use of active Self-Talk can make a difference, let's look at just a few of the circumstances in our careers and personal lives which can be helped or improved with the kind of Self-Talk we're discussing. The possibilities for using Self-Talk are limited only by the individual; there are as many uses as there are people with needs. Most of these examples, at some time and in some way, apply to all of us.

PUTTING SELF-TALK INTO PRACTICE

If you are in management: All of us are "managers" of one kind or another. There are two parts to good management. Effective management always begins with successful *self*-management. You can be a graduate student of management and never attain the essential skills of managing others if you do not first master the management of yourself. True leaders have their own selves firmly in control; they are in command of their actions, their feelings, their attitudes, and their perspectives.

The second essential ingredient of being a good manager is knowing how to develop the qualities and skills of others.

Both of these management requirements are directly affected by Self-Talk. If there are two equally qualified managers, similar in every respect, and one of them uses positive Self-Talk with himself or herself, and the other does not, and the same manager develops positive Self-Talk attitudes in his or her employees, and the other does not, which manager has the better chance of succeeding and which does not?

Managers have an exceptional opportunity to apply Self-Talk to nearly every situation they encounter, every business day. If you want your business to compete, grow, and prosper, put Self-Talk to work with your management team. Instead of replacing people, start replacing their internal "cannots" with capable, confident, self-belief. Self-Talk does that. And one of the areas it does it best is in managing others to get the right job done in the right way.

If you want to earn more income or improve your financial stability: Our earning potential is individually determined by each of us. The limits of our income are set by our own internal beliefs. If you want to earn more, you have to start by seeing yourself as worthy, deserving, capable, and willing—and by redirecting yourself to do so.

Too many of us, when we want to increase our earnings, make the mistake of tackling the problem from the wrong end. We try to figure out how we can earn more money before we believe we are capable of doing it. Talk to yourself about your self-worth. When you start to create a new picture of yourself being worth more, your subconscious mind will help you find a way to go about earning it. I don't want to over-simplify the task of making a significant increase in your financial net worth, but I have learned that doing so is far more dependent upon attitude, belief, and determination, than on the position you are presently in today.

If you are serious about wanting to increase your income, begin by giving yourself three weeks of Self-Talk for self-worth and financial worth—*then* set your goals and write your plan. When you determine who you really are *inside,* and what you are really capable of accomplishing, it is much easier to see what to do next. Start with your programming; the rest will follow.

If you raise children, teach them, or work with them in any way: A frequent story I hear is that of how the introduction of new Self-Talk in a home has affected the children. In most instances, it is one or both of the parents who begin using positive Self-Talk to work on some problem or to help them reach some of their goals. Since the use of Self-Talk in one area usually spreads to giving yourself the right kind of Self-Talk in other areas, it is not surprising that children, when they hear it used repeatedly in the home, begin to pick it up and use it almost accidentally.

It has always struck me how children accept positive Self-Talk *naturally,* even more easily than some of their parents. It can only be that as children we are still more willing to enthusiastically welcome anything which tells us the *good* things about ourselves. Our inner selves would far rather hear the best of who we can be than hear a daily discourse on the mistakes we make. Children are closer to the original potential we were born with. Until we become programmed to believe what we cannot do, as children we are still willing to believe in what we can.

CREATING A BETTER CHANCE
TO SUCCEED

Imagine a home in which one of two children was allowed and encouraged to listen to and learn positive Self-Talk, while the second child was not allowed to learn Self-Talk or benefit from it. If those two children were similar in other respects, imagine how each of them might respond differently to situations in their young lives.

What a child thinks about himself will affect how well he does in school, the kind of friends he chooses, how well he gets along with others, how he deals with the problems of teenage expectations, how he keeps himself in control when peer group pressure encourages him to take the wrong path, the kind of mate he will eventually choose, the kind of career he'll follow, and how well he will do in every big and small area of his life.

If there were two such children, one whose Self-Talk created strong self-esteem, good habits, and a positive "Yes I can!" spirit—and one who was left to rely on the average unsure programming most children receive, which one would you vote for? I would vote for the child with the winning self-belief. Along with the in-born characteristics handed down by heredity, the self-belief *is* the child. That young child *will become* what he believes about himself most.

Parents have asked me why their son or daughter has chosen the worst possible kind of friends to associate with. All of us, and perhaps teenagers especially, seek out others who we unconsciously believe we are most like. If a child has a less than positive picture of himself or herself, he or she will select those friends who are most like that picture—even if those friends are the wrong kind of friends. Give the child a better self-image, a better self-picture, and he will choose more of his friends from the group that fits the same kind of picture. If a teenager is told he's no good, and believes it, he'll find others who are just as no good, or worse.

Self-Talk can change that. Because Self-Talk changes the picture—*it changes the programming, which creates the belief, which develops the attitude, which creates the feelings, which control the behavior.* If you'd like your child to do the *right* things, start at the beginning. Start with his or her Self-Talk.

If you want to conquer a problem or overcome an obstacle: We've already discussed examples of Self-Talk for solving problems. A problem can be anything we want to conquer—large or small. You may want to use Self-Talk to resolve major dilemmas or simply to fix small past complaints. And in some cases, even a small amount of exactly the right Self-Talk will help you take a minor step that creates major results.

SIMPLE WORDS— IMPORTANT RESULTS

I received a call one day during a live radio talk show. The caller was a woman who told me and the listening audience that for two years she had not been able to get a job interview. Years earlier she had been a successful administrative assistant. She eventually quit working to stay home and raise a family. Now she wanted to go back to work, but during her time away she had lost all but the last vestige of her professional self-confidence. The more time went on, the more she became convinced that she would not be able to get a job. For two years she sat at home and talked herself into believing the worst.

She then told us that the reason she could not get a

job interview was because she couldn't get up the courage to make the phone call! Obviously, in a few brief minutes, I could not change her self-belief; she had worked too long and too hard destroying it to, in one moment, turn it around. But I could tell, just by listening to her story, that she really wanted to make a change. So I concentrated on the smallest, simplest step. I talked to her only about the Self-Talk it would take to dial *one* number—the first number of the telephone number she wanted to call to ask for an interview—and then the next number, and the next, and so on. She said she would try it, and we went on to another caller.

I was delighted, but not completely surprised, when, thirty minutes later, the last caller of the day was the same woman who had called with the job problem earlier in the program. She had done it. She had first dialed just one number, and then another. I had told her earlier that if she just took little steps, one push-button on the telephone at a time, that her next step would be just as simple. Just push the next button, and if she wanted to stop at any time, she could. But if pushing one button felt okay, go ahead, use the Self-Talk I had suggested to her, and push the next button.

I think all the listeners and I were silently applauding her when she told us that she had gotten through all seven digits of the phone number—for the first time in two years—and she was going to her first job interview at nine-thirty the next morning! I will never forget the sound in her voice. It was jubilation. It was, "I can do it. I *did it!*"

It was an incredibly small step. It took the smallest amount of the simplest words of positive Self-Talk. She did what she thought she couldn't do. She did it all by herself. And she changed in a positive and productive way, some of the most important years of her life. The Self-Talk may have been simple, but the *results* were profound.

If you want to reach goals: Setting good goals is one of the most important means to achieving them that I have ever found. Setting goals, and working at reaching them, is part and parcel to becoming healthy, wealthy, and wise; worthy goals are essential to true and lasting self-fulfillment.

Imagine setting worthwhile goals—and then fueling them with the non-stop energy of Self-Talk. You could achieve them without it perhaps, but the road would be harder. Give life to your dreams, give strength to your visions, give light to your path. Grant your journey the assurance of a safe arrival. Set your goals, work at achieving them, and talk to yourself every day along the way.

Setting goals and talking to yourself go hand in hand. But talk to yourself in exactly the right way and you will find the road easier to follow. If you are not yet setting goals—and writing them down—you should. If you are already an active goal-setter, give to your goals the gift of your own self-assurance. Add the words of daily direction and encouragement of Self-Talk to your goals, Any well-set goal deserves the benefit of well-said words.

If you want to improve your job: In one way or another we are all subject to the directions of others. We all have rules which we must follow. How you look at your job, your vocation, your associates and your employer, boss, or supervisor, will have an important effect on how well you do and how you feel about yourself in the job you are in. If you tell yourself that you do not like your job—you probably won't. If you tell yourself that you are unhappy with your manager or employer, you probably will be.

TAKING YOUR SELF-TALK TO WORK WITH YOU

Give yourself an advantage. Talk to yourself about your work and the people you work with in a way which makes your work *work* for you—and it will. You can decide to be happy with yourself and your job or you can decide to go home every night complaining about the things you don't like.

What do you suppose is the single most important difference between a happy, motivated employee and one for whom nothing ever works out right? It is entirely dependent on each employee's attitudes and feelings—both of which are entirely dependent on the individual's personal determination to view his or her work in a healthy, positive perspective—or not. Employees who "get the breaks" usually create them for themselves. Believe that you can reach your goals on the job, and you have just improved your chances of reaching those goals.

If you ever find yourself falling into the habit of finding fault with, complaining about, criticizing, or resenting your job, step aside and talk to yourself. There are others who have it far worse; some of them would love to have the opportunity which you now have.

Your job, or your occupation, does a lot more than pay the bills. It gives you the opportunity to excel, to expect the best of yourself and to put that expectation into practice. Your success will always depend on what you think, what you tell yourself most. Expect the best and then tell yourself the best. If you do, there is a good chance that that is what you will get.

If you'd like to do better in school—or any time you are improving your skills: You may not be in school at the moment, but if you are or if you ever plan to go back, your Self-Talk could be the deciding factor in how well you do in school—academically and personally. First off, Self-Talk can help you with the basics; it can help you listen better, have more concentration, help you develop and keep good study habits, improve your determination to stay with it, sharpen your memory, and help you keep your spirits up and your eye firmly fixed on the goal ahead.

Doing well in school or at learning anything is no different than achieving in any other part of life; the exact same attitudes, skills, and self-belief are required. But studying and learning do impose special demands that require special kinds of Self-Talk. There is no doubt that the program which operates your internal computer will have a direct affect on your scholastic success. If you could use some help, either in school or out, make sure your own computer has the program that is getting you where you want to go. Add Self-Talk to your curriculum. You'll get more from school and more from yourself.

If you ever get down, feel lonely, or become depressed: If things aren't going so well, it's time to change the program and start things looking up again! Using Self-Talk to deal with loneliness or depression is one of its best uses and one of the easiest to put into practice.

Because Self-Talk deals with you and what you think, it deals directly with the root of the problem. In the case of loneliness, it is more than Self-Talk's self-conversation which can help. It is true that some of the time you spend alone may be best spent engaged in a worthwhile conversation with yourself. But it is the reprogramming which the Self-Talk conversation creates that is most helpful in turning the experience of being alone into an experience that is positive and profitable.

WE CREATED IT—WE CAN CHANGE IT

Some believe that whatever we create in our lives, we can change. But changing it has been the hard part. The despair and despondency of depression are all too often a part of many of our lives.

But those kinds of depression which are self-created *can* be lightened or removed; the thoughts and the mood which caused them in the first place can be replaced—by the refreshing change of mental scenery which Self-Talk creates. Any of us can talk ourselves *into* depression and discouragement—and we can as easily talk ourselves *out* of it. It doesn't take an iron will or a special formula; it takes a new word-for-word program that will redirect our self-belief, an adjustment in our pictures of ourselves and what's going on around us.

It is our choice to see things any way we want to see them. If we want to view our circumstances as dark and discouraging, we can. If we would rather view our circumstances as acceptable, hopeful, changeable, and positively possible, we can. But it takes more than just *wanting* things to work out right. That's why things didn't work out right in the first place—we hadn't given ourselves the right pictures, the right input to create the right output. And that's something any of us can do something about.

When dealing with depression, counselors often recommend the right diet and the right physical activities to help counteract the depression. I would add to that recommendation a healthy diet of bright, new Self-Talk, and the daily activity of putting it to work.

THE OPPORTUNITIES TO USE SELF-TALK ARE UNLIMITED

If you would simply like to achieve: Each of us, everyone you or I could ever meet, would like to achieve *something*. For some of us it is to become better or achieve in only one or two areas of our lives. For others it is to achieve the best we can in every area. If you were to make a list of those parts of your life, those problems, circumstances, or opportunities which Self-Talk could help you overcome, deal with, or attain, the list could be almost endless. If you want to develop better self-esteem, get more done, change jobs, learn a new skill, become more creative, reduce stress, take better care of yourself, stop worrying, overcome depression, break through your limitations, get along better with others, or become more successful at anything, your own self-programmed Self-Talk lies at the root of your success.

Think of any job, career, position, task, or opportunity that comes to your mind. In any circumstance we might encounter, which of us has the better chance of succeeding? Those of us who have given ourselves the extra benefit of self-assurance and determination—overriding our fears and charging past our obstacles—or those of us who resist our potentials, hang on to our old programming, and live with uncertainty, doubt, and disbelief?

Which would you rather do? Imagine for a moment any problem you would like to overcome, right now, or any change you would like to make in yourself or in your life. If there were two of you, and one of you became a positive, productive Self-Talker, and the other did not, for whom would you cast your vote? I know which one I would vote for, every time.

CHAPTER SIXTEEN

Changing Habits

OF THE MANY WAYS you can use Self-Talk in its various forms, you will find that all Self-Talk suggestions or phrases fit into one of four categories: *Habit-Changing, Attitude-Building, Motivational,* or *Situational* Self-Talk.

Most of us have a habit or two that we would like to change. It is usually something we do that causes us problems (or causes other people problems). These are the habits that get in our way, hold us back, or in some cases, stop us completely—they are the well-trodden paths which, even though they lead us in the wrong direction, we most easily follow.

All habits are the result of our previous conditioning—things we learned to do, and then practiced them until they became what seems like a natural way to behave. They are not natural at all, of course; we weren't born with any of them. They are habits—negative programs that stuck. Any of them can be replaced with a new program.

"Habit-Changing" Self-Talk helps you work on a specific problem. This is the Self-Talk that directs your subconscious mind to stop doing something one way and start doing it another. It is the Self-Talk which replaces a behavior pattern that works against you with a behavior pattern which helps you solve problems or reach goals by changing your actions—specific things that you do which you would rather not be doing, and specific things which you would rather do, but have not been doing. Let's look at a few of the more common habits with which all of us are familiar:

Putting Things Off Or Procrastinating
Smoking
Working Too Hard Or Not Working Hard
    Enough
Arguing
Ignoring Problems
Over-Sleeping
Forgetting Names Or Other Important Things
Being A Complainer
Making Excuses
Losing Things
Overindulging—Eating Or Drinking Too Much
Being Sarcastic
Saying "Yes" When You Want To Say "No"
Never Being On Time
Not Listening
Blaming Others
Interrupting Other People When They're Talking
Being Disorganized
Not Telling The Truth
Worrying
Being A Gossip
Not Setting Priorities
Letting Your Emotions Control You

Wasting Time
Giving Advice That Isn't Asked For
Spending More Money Than You Earn
Talking Too Much
Being Overly Critical of Others
Not Taking Care Of Details
Starting Something But Not Finishing It

All of these are habits—I'm sure you could add a few more to the list—and all of them can be changed or improved upon with the right kind of Self-Talk.

Whether a habit you would like to change is as simple as stopping smoking or getting something done on time, there is a specific kind of Self-Talk which will help you do just that. Habit-changing Self-Talk is specific and demanding. It refuses to tolerate or accept the *old* habit while it creates a new picture of you acting and behaving in a way which puts the old habit behind you; it puts you into motion with a productive new habit pattern which replaces the old.

PUT YOUR SELF-TALK
IN THE PRESENT

All positive Self-Talk (with the exception of Situational Self-Talk, which we will discuss later) is written, read, recorded, listened to, thought, and spoken in the *present tense*. It is always stated as though the desired change *has already taken place*. By doing this you are giving your subconscious mind a completed picture of the accomplished task; you are presenting your control center with the command which says, "This is the me I want you to create for me." The more finished or complete the picture, the more specific the directions you are giving your subconscious mind will be.

When you want to give a new directive to your subconscious you would not say, as an example, "I'm *going* to lose weight." When you say "I'm going to . . .," what are you actually telling your control center? "Tomorrow, later, some other time, I'll lose weight in the future ('I'm *going* to'), but for now, keep me like I am." And tomorrow never comes.

If you tell yourself, "*I will, I'm going to, I need to, I should, I'd like to, I want to,*" or "*I wish I could,*" I don't doubt that your subconscious will believe you: it just won't do anything about it!

State your goal or the result you want to achieve in the present tense. Because the subconscious mind does not know what is true and what is not, in time it will accept what you are telling it and act on it. But remember, it will attempt to follow the *exact* wording of the directions you are giving it:

> *I always do everything I need to do, when I need to do it.*
>
> *I never argue or let my emotions work against me.*
>
> *I don't smoke!*
>
> *I have a good memory. I easily and automatically remember any name or anything that is important to me.*
>
> *I eat only what I should.*
>
> *I am a good listener—I hear everything that is said—I am attentive, interested, and aware of everything that is going on around me.*

I have the courage to state my opinions. I take responsibility for myself and everything I say and do.

I never spend more than I earn. I am financially responsible, both for my present and for my future.

I set goals and I follow them. I set my sights, take the appropriate action, and achieve my goals.

I spend time with my family and my loved ones. I enjoy sharing their lives with mine and my life with theirs.

Each of these examples of positive Self-Talk deals directly with "habits"—preconditioned styles of behavior which frustrate us or hold us back. In each case, each of the examples states the change in the present tense, as though the desired result has already taken place, but each example states only a single Self-Talk phrase or two out of many which, in actual practice, you would use to create the change you want to make.

When you are using Self-Talk to change a habit, effect an attitude, or create internal motivation, it works most effectively when you build a solid body of Self-Talk around the subject you are working on. One phrase of the right kind of Self-Talk can have an effect on your behavior, but it is only when you paint an *entirely new picture* for your subconscious mind that you will derive the full benefit from your Self-Talk.

If you were to choose one of the examples we just used, and wanted to change an old habit by using just *one* Self-Talk phrase only, no matter how often you repeated that bit of Self-Talk, it would have only limited results. But start with that one phrase and extend it, add to it, cover every part of the problem by including Self-Talk phrases, Self-Talk suggestions which cover every hidden corner.

Remember, your new Self-Talk is the navigation system that you are using to chart your new destination, and determine your course, direction, altitude, and speed. So be specific and be thorough. Don't expect vague directions, hints of solutions, and shadows of expectations to get you where you're going.

GET SPECIFIC

When you use Self-Talk, leave no stone unturned. Isolate the problem, look at it from every angle, make a list of every area *within that problem,* and add a line of Self-Talk to cover it. While I have found few problems which can be solved with a single phrase or two of Self-Talk, I have found that in most cases any specific problem, no matter how large, or any goal, no matter how important, can be covered with as few as a dozen or so well-chosen Self-Talk suggestions.

Let's use an example of the individual whose goal it is to quit smoking. We'll use that example because smoking is one of those habits which everyone recognizes as just that—a "habit," even though each of the other examples I've given is just as much a "habit" as is smoking. We could as easily use an example of someone who wants to stop the habit of procrastinating, arguing less at home, or wasting precious time doing nothing instead of doing something worthwhile.

However, even if you don't smoke, you should be able to adapt the following Self-Talk example to anything *you* would like to work on for yourself.

You should, by reading these few phrases of Self-Talk, very quickly recognize that Self-Talk is not one simple phrase or two: *Self-Talk is a specific set of concisely worded directions—usually a group of a dozen or more combined phrases, linked together on the same subject, which jointly paint a detailed picture of the better you which you would like to become, or the change in your life you would like to create.*

In this example the old habit has been supported with daily negative Self-Talk—the kind we talked about earlier: "No matter what I do I can't seem to quit smoking," "Smoking helps me relax," or "When I stop smoking I gain weight." That's the old programming. But the new *habit-changing* Self-Talk looks at all of those things differently.

In the following Self-Talk, watch every phrase for the picture it presents; note the instructions that are being given, word-for-word, to the subconscious mind of the individual who used to think that smoking was an appropriate thing to do.

POSITIVE SELF-TALK TO STOP SMOKING

I do not smoke. My lungs are strong and healthy. I am able to breathe deeply and fully.

Taking care of myself physically is important to me. I like keeping myself fit and feeling good.

I am a non-smoker—and I am proud of myself.

I have more energy and stamina than ever before. I enjoy life and I'm glad to be here.

When I see a cigarette, or even think of one, I automatically hear the words, "I do not smoke"— and I don't!

I have no habits which control or influence me in any harmful way. I am in control of myself and everything I do. I always do what is best for me, myself, and my future.

I really enjoy breathing clean, fresh air, being healthy, and being in complete control of my body and my mind.

I am able to achieve any goal which I set for myself. I see, in my mind, a clear picture of myself having already accomplished my goal. I create it, I see it often, and I achieve it.

I exercise regularly. I keep myself fit and healthy. And I am enjoying a lifetime of energy and vitality.

All of my senses are clear and alive. My sight, my sense of smell, my hearing, my tasting, and even my touch are more alive than ever before.

I do not see smoking as being strong, intelligent, or glamorous in any way. I see it for what it really is, and it has no place in my life.

I give myself permission to relax, feel good, breathe deeply and fully, and enjoy being a healthy non-smoker at all times and in all circumstances.

People enjoy being around me. I have self-confidence and self-respect. I like myself, and it shows!

Being a non-smoker is easy for me. After all, I

was born that way—and it is the natural thing for me to do.

If you *are* a smoker and would like to quit, try reading those words to your subconscious mind three or four times a day for the next three weeks and watch what happens. I suspect that you will find, as many others have, that the new directions you are giving yourself could have an alarming impact on the old program you had become used to. The old habits, in anything we do, are nothing more than the old programming we accepted and got used to.

If you would like to change an old habit, seek out your old programming, recognize it for what it is, make a minor decision to do something about it, and erase it and replace it with something better.

Let's look at another example of Habit-Changing Self-Talk. In this instance we'll use Self-Talk to tackle a habit that holds a lot of people back from reaching their full potential—the habit of wasting time on worry. Conquering just this one negative habit has turned underachievers into winners and given them extra time, peace of mind, and a fresh new outlook on life.

Once again, when you read the examples of habit-changing Self-Talk, notice that the Self-Talk doesn't just talk about the symptoms—it breaks the old habit down and gets at its roots. The positive new Self-Talk covers the problem from every angle. It creates a completely new, better mental environment. It shows you a natural, new picture of yourself actually *being* the worry-free, more productive person you would like to become.

This time, as you read the Self-Talk, try reading it out loud. Make it more than a few words written in the pages of a book. Give it life. Self-Talk becomes active when you pull it off the written page and address it directly to yourself.

POSITIVE SELF-TALK FOR FREEDOM FROM WORRY

I do not worry. I am in control of my own thinking and I think only those thoughts which create and fulfill the best in me.

My mind is constantly in tune with the positive. It is bright, cheerful, enthusiastic, and full of good, positive thoughts and ideas.

I am able to relax easily and comfortably in my body and in my mind. I am calm, confident, and self-assured.

My mind is orderly and well-organized. I consciously choose what I think and I always choose those thoughts which are the most positive and beneficial for me.

All of my thoughts create healthiness within me.

My mind dwells only on those thoughts which create more harmony, balance, and well-being within me and in the world around me.

I automatically, and always, think in a decisive and determined way.

I am full of resolution and the absolute assurance of the best possible outcome in everything that I do.

I choose to look at the world around me in the bright, healthy light of optimism and self-assurance.

I do only those things which are best for me. I create the best within myself, I attract the best in others, and I find the best in the world around me.

I willingly, and without fail, take care of the duties and obligations which I have accepted for myself.

I commit only to those responsibilities which I know I can fulfill.

I focus the attention of my mind only on those things that I can do something about. If I cannot affect it or direct it—I accept it.

I keep my mind too busy thinking good, healthy, positive, constructive, and productive thoughts to ever have any time for worry.

I control the thoughts I choose. No thought, at any time, can dwell in my mind without my approval or permission.

I never worry.

For every habit you can come up with that should be changed, there is the right Self-Talk to change it. But the two examples of habit-changing Self-Talk we have just seen will give you an idea of how Self-Talk is constructed and how it covers not only the problem itself, but how it creates the surrounding mental *environment* that feeds and supports the decision to change.

Most of those things we call bad habits are in reality the symptoms of something else which is going on inside of us. They are the result of a broad variety of beliefs we have about ourselves which, when all lumped together, push us into a pattern of behavior which ends up causing problems for us. Self-Talk looks at the "whole being" (all of the furniture in our mental apartments) from a holistic point of view. It doesn't just cure the symptom, it changes the problems which *caused* the symptoms in the first place.

TO CHANGE THE HABIT, CHANGE THE WORDS

We *are* creatures of habit. But any habit once learned can be changed. The problem has been that in the past, changing them has been difficult because we were trying to change direction without first changing the old programming. With Self-Talk we accomplish both: we override the old while we are creating the new.

Choose a habit you would like to change. Don't try to change your life overnight—start off with a minor habit, something small. Then change the words which describe yourself to you. Once you begin, keep at it. It is exciting to watch the changes that take place, to witness the replacement of old habits which once got in the way, with the emergence of fruitful, valuable new habits of winning.

CHAPTER SEVENTEEN

Changing Attitudes

EVERYTHING WE DO is affected directly or indirectly by our attitudes. A change in a person's attitude can affect just about everything else in that person's life. Even a small shift in "attitude adjustment" can have a profound effect on what we do and how we do it. If you have ever had a son or daughter in school, you know how true that is. A change in attitude can result in a change in grades, dress, habits, and friends.

The better the attitude, the better the results, in almost anything we do. Because attitude affects our feelings and feelings affect what we do and how well we do it, having a good attitude can be the deciding factor in our successes or failures. The right attitude gives us that important edge.

Since our attitudes are the result of our programming, it makes good sense to take a look at the attitudes we are living with, why they are what they are, and which of them we might like to change. Because every attitude we have *directly* affects how we feel about everything around us and what we do about it—our attitudes are *important!* Without the right attitudes we will *never* have the key that unlocks the treasure chest of happiness and success we so badly want and so richly deserve.

Attitudes create the biggest part of the picture we see of ourselves. They are the filters through which we view everything in our sight. Our attitudes are our dispositions—they are the "state of mind" we live in. Our attitudes express themselves through our moods, our temperament, our willingness, and our hesitations.

Our attitudes propel us forward toward our victories or bog us down in defeat. They are the foothold beneath us in every step we take. They are what others see most of the personality within us; they describe us and define us, projecting the image we present to the world around us. Our attitudes make us rich or poor, happy or unhappy, fulfilled or incomplete. They are the single most determining factor in every action we will ever make. We and our attitudes are inextricably combined; *we* are our attitudes and our attitudes are *us*.

MANAGING ATTITUDES IN OTHERS

If you are in any way responsible for the development of the attitudes of others—as a manager, parent, teacher, or friend—don't expect to change someone else's attitude with "a carrot or a stick" by using incentives, lectures, punishment, complaints, or flattery. Attitudes don't work that way!

For years business managers have used incentives to boost attitudes to improve productivity or increase sales. But even though they get short-term improvements, the same businesses find that before too long they have to put a new incentive program into effect. They didn't really change any attitudes. They did nothing more than create a short-term, temporary effect in their employees' *outward behavior*—not a change in their attitudes.

If you use an incentive of one kind or another to change an attitude, it may *appear* to work, but the effect won't last; you will find yourself needing to resupply another incentive each time the previous incentive wears off.

Another time that we frequently use the wrong method to change attitudes is when we are attempting to help someone else improve an attitude that we believe is working against that person. In spite of the fact that school counselors, parents, husbands, wives, managers, and friends frequently tell some individual, "You need to change your attitude," telling someone that has never done any good at all. In fact, just saying that to someone can have the wrong effect—it is negative programming—it will work against the individual instead of for him. It *reconfirms* his preprogrammed belief that all the bad things he already thinks about himself are true! In fact, it is precisely when a person's attitude is "down" that it is the hardest for that person to figure out any way to change it! Why should they? How can they?

Our attitudes are determined by our beliefs—and if we believe we are less than the best, to us that is *fact!*, that is reality—that's the way it *is!* Of course, it isn't true at all. It's just true to the person who believes it.

Recall for a moment the natural process by which attitudes are created in each of us: "Programming creates beliefs, beliefs create attitudes, attitudes create feelings, feelings determine actions, and actions create results." Each of those steps—behavior, feelings, attitude, and beliefs—is the logical and expected result of our conditioning. It follows then that every attitude we have, good, bad, or indifferent, is the natural result of the programming that preceded it.

Every one of us from time to time suffers from a less than perfect attitude. A "bad attitude" doesn't belong solely to the student who won't study or to the company employee who didn't get a raise or to the best friend whose personal life has just fallen apart. Attitudes, good and bad, are an everyday part of our lives.

CHANGING ATTITUDES IN YOURSELF

An attitude we might like to change need not be an attitude that is calamitous or extreme—it may be a problem which is quite simple, an attitude which, if fine tuned just a little, could make some small part of our daily lives work better. And because even the simplest or the most important of our attitudes can be changed by redoing a piece or two of our programming, if we would like to make the change—and we know how to make that programming change—there really isn't any impassable obstacle stopping us from going ahead and doing it.

The attitudes which you have about yourself create one additional important result: the attitudes you have about yourself determine the attitudes you will have about everything else around you. So if you want to change the way you feel about anything else, you have to start first with the attitudes you have about yourself.

It is for this reason that most of the Attitude-Changing Self-Talk deals with *you*—and how you see yourself. To illustrate, let's examine an actual pre-written script of attitude-changing Self-Talk. This category of Self-Talk includes such subject titles as "Freedom From Worry," "Taking Responsibility For Yourself," "Building Self-Esteem," "Positive Self-Talk For Teens," "Overcoming Obstacles," "Determination And Will Power," "Successful Marriage," "Overcoming Personal Limitations," and "Believing In Incredible You."

For this example we'll use a Self-Talk script for "personal responsibility." Our attitudes about the part each of us plays in our own earthly destinies are some of the most important attitudes we will ever hold. The difference between having an attitude of accepting responsibility for who we are and what we do, and having an attitude which makes excuses or places our lives in the hands of others, is essential to our ability to achieve a sense of "self," and the individual fulfillment which self-responsibility creates within us.

But even considering the importance which this one atttiude plays in each of our lives, notice how directly, and effectively, even a few Self-Talk statements can address a subject, simplify it, and begin the reprogramming process of an attitude that is essential to all of us:

SELF-TALK FOR TAKING RESPONSIBILITY FOR YOURSELF

I take full responsibility for everything about me—even the thoughts that I think. I am in control of the vast resources of my own mind.

I alone am responsible for what I do and what I

tell myself about me. No one can share this responsibility with me.

I also allow others to accept their responsibilities for themselves and I do not try to accept their responsibilities for them.

I enjoy being responsible. It puts me in charge of being me—and that's a challenge I enjoy.

I allow no one else, at any time, to assume control or responsibility over my life or over anything that I do. My responsibility to others is an extension of my own responsibility to myself.

I choose to leave nothing about me up to chance. When it comes to me—and anything in my life—I choose to CHOOSE!

My choices are mine alone to make for myself. I do not, at any time, allow anyone else to make my choices for me. And I accept full responsibility for every choice and decision I make.

I always meet all of the obligations which I accept. And I accept no obligations which I will not meet.

I am trustworthy. I can be counted on. I have accepted winning responsibility for myself—and I always live up to the responsibilities I accept.

There is no they on whom I lay the blame, or with whom I share my own personal responsibilities. I have learned the great secret of mastering my own destiny. I have learned that "they" is "me!"

I have no need to make excuses and no one needs

to carry my responsibility for me. I gladly carry my own weight—and I carry it well.

Each day I acknowledge and accept the responsibility not only for my own actions—but also for my emotions, my thoughts, and my attitudes.

I accept the responsibility for living my life in a way which creates my strengths, my happiness, my positive, healthy beliefs, and for my past, my present, and my future.

That's a good attitude!—the kind of attitude which most of us could do with a little more of. It is an attitude which gets us to stand up for ourselves and be counted! It is an attitude which we can, if we choose, effect in our own lives any time we want. But it is just one attitude of many which each of us can address and put into motion just by reconvincing ourselves—by overriding the old programming which told us that other people, by some stroke of fate, count more than we do.

There are many such attitudes. Some of them are less lofty, and perhaps not as demanding. But they are made up of perhaps the most important Self-Talk of all—the Self-Talk of self-*belief*. That is what attitudes are all about.

Here is an example of attitude-changing Self-Talk which any of us could use from time to time. If I were ever again to teach in a classroom, I would add the lesson of this Self-Talk to my everyday curriculum. It is one of the most basic and primary forms of Self-Talk. But the attitude it can create in us touches every part of our lives. It is the fabric of which all success is woven. It is the God-given birthright which all of us were born with, and deserve to retrieve, embrace, enjoy, and possess for the rest of our lives. It restores us and builds us up. It structures our character, sustains our strength, and fortifies our courage. It is the internal substance of self-belief—it is the Self-Talk of *self-esteem*:

SELF-TALK FOR BUILDING SELF-ESTEEM

I really am very special. I like who I am and I feel good about myself.

Although I always work to improve myself and I get better every day, I like who I am today. And tomorrow, when I'm even better, I'll like myself then, too!

It's true that there really is no one else like me in the entire world. There never was another me before, and there will never be another me again.

I am unique—from the top of my head to the bottom of my feet. In some ways I may look and act and sound like some others—but I am not them. I am me.

I wanted to be somebody—and now I know I am. I would rather be me than anyone else in the world.

I like how I feel and I like how I think and I like how I do things. I approve of me and I approve of who I am.

I have many beautiful qualities about me. I have talents and skills and abilities. I even have talents that I don't even know about yet. And I am discovering new talents inside myself all the time.

I am positive. I am confident. I radiate good things. If you look closely, you can even see a glow around me.

I am full of life. I like life and I'm glad to be alive. I am a very special person, living at a very special time.

I am intelligent. My mind is quick and alert and clever and fun. I think good thoughts, and my mind makes things work right for me.

I have a lot of energy and enthusiasm and vitality. I am exciting and I really enjoy being me.

I like to be around other people and other people like to be around me. People like to hear what I have to say and know what I have to think.

I smile a lot. I am happy on the inside and I am happy on the outside.

I am interested in many things. I appreciate all the blessings I have, and the things that I learn, and all the things I will learn today and tomorrow and forever—just as long as I am.

I am warm, sincere, honest, and genuine. I am all of these things and more. And all of these things are me. I like who I am, and I'm glad to be me!

What simple words they are. What truths they tell us about the selves we contain inside of us. Placed within the beliefs of any one individual, those simple words possess a power which few of us have ever hoped to attain. And yet that self-belief, that sense of self-esteem is available to all of us. Can you imagine living that way each day—and knowing it?

Imagine children growing up with those kinds of words indelibly instilled in their believing, eager young minds. Imagine the world *they* could create. But for today, for now, just imagine beginning to believe the very best about yourself, each day, all of the time, in any circumstance, always being sure of attitudes that support you, give you faith, prop you up, and give you the courage and the conviction to live life in its most fulfilling, most positive way.

If that sounds improbable, let me remind you that it is your *old* programming that tells you it can't work that way. That is because that is what it was programmed to believe. And it is wrong.

TAKE STOCK OF YOUR ATTITUDES

Look at your attitudes. Assess them, examine them. Take stock of your beliefs about yourself, take a mental inventory of your attitudes—good and bad— and decide for yourself which of those attitudes work for you and which do not. The ones you don't want to keep—throw out. Get rid of them. Keep the ones you like. Change the ones you want to change. Take charge of your attitudes. Put yourself back in control. The least that could happen is that you would get a little more of your real self back again.

Start the adventure. Discover the jewels and gems that are part of your own mind. Seek out and find the rich reserve of the "attitudes" within you which have been waiting to step out and live again. Start talking to yourself the *right* way.

Little changes in attitudes can make big changes in

life. Your attitudes affect all of the important things around you. They affect how you feel about yourself. They affect your work, your friends, and your loved ones. When your attitudes get better, so does life. If you would like to make a change or two, fixing an attitude and making life a little better isn't a bad place to start.

CHAPTER EIGHTEEN

Solving Problems and Accomplishing Goals

THERE IS A kind of Self-Talk which, although it has a positive effect on our habits and our attitudes, is used specifically to fix problems or help us reach our goals. Problems and goals often go hand in hand. "Problems" are usually thought of as those things which get in the way of our goals. For a moment, replace the word "problem" with the word "challenge": Goals create challenges—and challenges create goals.

The Self-Talk that will help you solve your problems is the same Self-Talk that will help you reach your goals. To the brain, overcoming problems and accomplishing goals are one and the same. To your subconscious mind, seeing yourself overcoming a challenge, solving a problem, and reaching a goal, the exact same set of directions are required—the Self-Talk is the same.

While I do agree that the mind looks at what we call "problems" and what we call "goals" in exactly the same way, I do not agree with those who tell us that all problems are "opportunities." Some problems represent potential opportunities, but not all of them. If a man with a gun in his hand were to walk in at this moment and point the gun at your head, that is *not* an opportunity—that is a *problem!*

Just by understanding that the subconscious mind recognizes, accepts, and acts on problems in the exact same way that it helps us reach our goals, we can change, in a positive way, how we look at many of those things in our lives that we have been told are the natural circumstances of life, which, when overcome, automatically and naturally result in the achievement of goals. *You cannot solve a problem without reaching an objective.*

THE TRUE MEANING OF "GOALS"

If we want to talk to ourselves in the most productive way, we should also understand the true meaning of the word "goal." It is a word which has been badly misused. It has been given a position of power which it does not deserve. The more deeply I delved into the literature and teachings of self-improvement, the more I began to recognize that there were a number of words in our language, which had been redefined by a small body of authors, to hold an exalted status which the words themselves were not due.

As an example, even the wonderful word "Success" too many times has been used to mean "winning" rather than playing, being wealthy, being Number One, or driving an expensive foreign car and living in an exclusive neighborhood. That's not what success means at all. We know that. But because we have been told time and time again what success is, many individuals who have been successful in their own way, mistook that soaring definition as the correct definition. As a result they saw themselves as "failing," rather than succeeding.

So, too, has the word "Goal" been misused, misinterpreted, and misunderstood. The word goal is a word which has become so encumbered with priorities and demands that it makes even the thought of "setting and reaching goals" something of such great importance that we gladly see it as a task which others, possibly more dedicated than ourselves, might undertake, or something we set aside for another day when we have more time to think about it.

Setting goals should be simple. There is nothing wrong with aspiring to reach the highest mountains of "success." But when we set our sights on our great aspirations, we should never fail to recognize the little goals which get us there—the goals which we set almost *unconsciously,* day after day, which help us survive, endure, overcome, maintain, and achieve— each day, step by step. They are our wants, our needs, our smallest expectations of ourselves. These are some of the most important goals of all; they are the goals of everyday living.

Our goals should not be limited to setting short-term, medium-term, and long-term objectives. Although the right Self-Talk can help you reach the loftiest goals you can imagine, for most of us being President or becoming a millionaire is not the kind of goal we deal with on Monday morning.

You may have a goal as practical as losing a little extra weight, doing better at work, getting a promotion, earning more income or saving more of what you earn, getting past depression, getting more organized, writing better business plans, or closing more sales.

YOUR GOALS CAN BE ANYTHING YOU CHOOSE

Goals can be as important or as simple as having more free time, attending church more regularly, running a better household, getting good grades, having better personal relationships, being healthier, going to the symphony, writing a letter home, sending flowers a little more often, doing something special for someone else, looking good for the class reunion, smiling more often, conquering your slice in golf, or catching more fish.

Your goals, and the problems standing between you and those goals, can be anything at all, large or small. But your subconscious mind deals with all of them in the same matter-of-fact and accepting way. If you want to achieve them, give yourself the right directions, the right words—take advantage of your own mind's natural dedication to do for you what you tell it most.

To solve any problem or reach any goal, great or small, the internal mental process we go through is the same. If you want to be better at your job, lose weight, or create wealth in your life, it is all the same to your subconscious mind. To it, one direction is the same as any other. The more programming it receives to help you reach the objective you present it with, the more it will move in that direction.

To illustrate, before we target a specific problem or goal, let's look at an example of some Self-Talk which addresses the broader area of how we look at problems in general—what we *believe* about the problems we encounter in any given day. How we look at our problems plays an important role in what we do about them. Do we analyze, avoid, confront, go around them—or solve them?

It doesn't make any difference to our internal computer what the problem is or how big it is. But what we tell ourselves about our problems will affect every action we take from that moment forward.

SOLVING PROBLEMS

The following are a few words of Self-Talk for how to deal with the problem of "solving problems":

I'm good at solving problems. I like challenges and I meet them head on.

Problems are my teachers. They help me to learn and grow. Without them, I would be going nowhere. With them, I am moving forward in the direction of my own goals.

There is no problem which I cannot conquer. I am strong in mind, body, and spirit. My will, my strength, and my determination are always greater than any problem I face.

When I meet a new problem, I do not see the problem as my enemy. I know that finding the solution to the problem will move me forward in my own personal growth.

Because I know that problems are a key ingredient in my spiritual and mental education and preparation, I recognize that all problems are important to me.

I do not fear problems, I solve them. I do not ignore problems, I confront them. I do not avoid problems, I conquer them!

I know that every problem holds within itself the keys to its own solution. Therefore, the better I understand the problem, the clearer I am able to see its solution.

Having problems is not a problem for me. I am confident, self-assured, positive, and determined. I always know that I am going to overcome any problem I encounter—and I always do.

I am good at breaking large obstacles down into smaller pieces that are easier to handle. And I never make any problem appear to be larger than it actually is.

I never worry. I turn "worry time" into positive, constructive, "solution time." I keep my mind alert and open to all solutions—and solutions come quickly and easily to me.

I have learned to recognize that many problems carry with them benefits and potential opportunities which would not have presented themselves had the problem not occurred in the first place.

I do not seek to live a life which is free from all problems. Instead, I choose to live a life of finding solutions and enjoying the benefits which those solutions create.

Challenge, conquer, solution, and win are words which I live by daily. "Challenges" are opportunities. "Conquering them" is the inevitable outcome. "Solutions" are the stepping stones to my success, and "Winning" is my way of life.

I suspect you will find, as others have, that if you were to do nothing more than read that one example of a Self-Talk Script to yourself three or four times each day for a week or two, by the end of that time you would begin to see your own problems differently even though the examples of Self-Talk we have just used do not tackle a specific problem. It deals only with your general approach to looking at problems.

Now let's be more specific. Let's identify a problem—one which for many of us has, at one time or another, stood directly in the way of reaching almost any goal we set for ourselves: the problem of "being organized"—managing our time and our resources in a more effective and productive way.

There are a number of excellent books on the subject of managing time and becoming more organized. Think what those books could teach us if we first created an "internal environment" of organization and personal control. Before we attempt to use the techniques which solve the symptoms, imagine creating a new internal program which builds a new, more organized self-concept! There are excellent systems and methods for getting organized, managing time, and being more productive, which are available to anyone who wants to take the time to read a book or two on the subject.

But when you read the books on managing your time or becoming more organized, think how much better the soil of an *accepting* mind would be—a mind that has become reprogrammed, firmly convinced, regardless of what you might have believed in the past, to now believe that being "organized" is a *natural* way for you to be.

If your goal were to organize your thoughts, your time, and your activities to get more done for you, and help you reach the rest of the goals you have set for yourself instead of following the old programming, it is just as easy and far more effective to use a different set of internal commands:

I am organized and in control of my life. I am in control of myself, my thoughts, my time, my actions, and my future.

I know what to do and when to do it, and I do everything I need to do, when I need to do it.

I program my mind to make the maximum use of my time. I am in control of my time and how to use it. I like being organized, efficient, and on top of things. Controlling my time keeps me that way.

I never waste time—I always "plan" time. And because I plan my time I always have time to do the things I choose to do.

Each day I become more organized and in control of all areas of my life—at home, at work, in my mind and in my thoughts, in everything that I do.

I am very well organized. Each night I make a list of things I need to do the next day. I set my priorities and I follow them.

I am always on time. I am always right where I need to be, exactly when I need to be there. Being on time is easy for me and the more I control my time and the more organized I become, the easier it is.

I am in control of my feelings, my emotions, my attitudes, and my needs. I control them; they do not control me.

I have the winning vote in the outcome of my own actions. And I choose to live my life by choice, not chance. Therefore, I take the time to take control.

I have an organized and orderly mind. Because I think in an organized way, I conduct my life in an organized manner.

I think in the most positive and productive way at all times and in all things. The way I think is the way I live—and I think "right."

I am the director of my destiny. I know where I am going and I know why I am going there. My earthly life is in my hands and in my control.

I control my goals and the achievement of my goals. I organize my goals by writing each of them down, along with the steps I need to reach them. One of the reasons for my success is that my goals are clearly defined and organized.

I am in complete control of what I think and how I think. Therefore, I choose to think only those thoughts which help me and which are of genuine benefit to me.

Even after years of using Self-Talk for myself—by

writing, reading, recording, listening to, and putting Self-Talk into practice, and by talking with other people who use the same kind of Self-Talk for themselves—I am still impressed with the value and importance of its directness: the more simple and to the point your Self-Talk is, the better it works.

When I was working on the cassette tapes for "Self-Talk for Weight-Loss," the importance of using explicit, direct wording proved to be essential. While writing the actual Self-Talk for the problem (or the goal) of losing weight and keeping it off permanently, I identified *fourteen* individual subject areas of Self-Talk—each of which was vital to the one specific problem I was writing about. The list of weight-loss subjects included such areas as "Getting Started— Mentally," "Will Power," "Being Healthy and Feeling Good," "Sitting Down to Eat," "Controlling Between-Meal Snacks," "Hiding Behind Your Weight," "Getting Past Weight-Loss Barriers," and "Keeping Weight Off."

Each of the fourteen subject areas covered required a necessary and important Self-Talk script that dealt directly with that one important area of the problem. Each of the "scripts" was written to deal with every part and facet of that area of the problem. The individual scripts covered all of the details which had contributed to creating the overall problem. The importance of this is that your own personal Self-Talk should be simple, but it *must be direct, and it must deal with every facet of the problem or goal you are working on.*

To give you an example of how explicit and direct the right kind of Self-Talk should be, I'll give you a few of the actual Self-Talk self-directions from just one of those fourteen Self-Talk scripts that were written for the subject of weight-loss. This particular segment deals with a problem—and a goal—that everyone who has ever had a problem with weight has had to deal with at one time or another; the problem of "Sitting Down to Eat." It begins with the important self-direction of being in control, and then dives into the *details* of the problem:

I am in control of myself in every way—at all times and in all situations.

Each time I sit down to eat I reaffirm my determination to achieve my goal. By eating right, and never giving in, I am reaching the weight I want.

Whether eating in or eating out, I really enjoy eating less.

I never feel the need to finish the food in front of me. I eat only what I should—and never one bite more.

One way to weight-loss that's easy and works, is less food on my plate, and less on my fork!

By ordering less when I eat out, and by serving myself smaller portions at home, I keep myself aware of the importance of staying with my goal—each and every day. "Less on my plate means less on my waist."

When I sit down to eat, at no time do I allow anyone else to influence, tempt, or discourage me in any negative way.

What I eat, and the goals I reach, are up to me. And I give no one the right to hinder or control my success.

183

Although others may benefit from my success, I am achieving my weight-loss goals for my own personal reasons—for myself, my life, my future, and my own personal well-being.

I am never, at any time, tempted to take one bite more than I should. I am strong, I am capable of reaching my goal, and I am doing it!

Being in situations which put a lot of food in front of me is not a problem to me now. I simply say "No!" to the food and "Yes!" to my success.

I enjoy sitting down to eat. Each time I do I conquer my past, and I create a trimmer, happier, more self-confident future in front of me.

When I sit down to eat, I do not need someone else to remind me of my goal, or to keep me from eating something I should not. I take full responsibility for myself, and no one else has to do it for me.

Controlling my weight, and my appetite, is easy for me now. I enjoy smaller portions, smaller bites, and a slower, healthier, more relaxed way of eating.

I have set my goal and I am staying with it. I have turned mealtime into "achievement time."

That is the kind of healthy new Self-Talk which, when practiced even for a short period of time, begins to automatically step in to replace the earlier self-talk which kept us from reaching the goal we wanted to reach. Once you become conditioned to making that simple shift in what you say to yourself, the new self-directions come without thinking about them.

BE SPECIFIC—FIX THE PROBLEM

The key to good Self-Talk is that it covers the problem—and it gets specific! Broad, generalized "affirmations" of well-being are fine when you are working on creating a broad, generalized attitude. But when you want to fix a problem, *fix the problem!* When you want to achieve precise goals, even the little ones, *give yourself precise commands*.

That is why the idea of repeating "affirmations" to yourself has made sense, but the words which are so often used to construct the self-talk of affirmations have, in the past, too often dealt with *general* concepts instead of precise, immediate programming which would have a direct effect on our habits, attitudes, problems, and goals each day.

A few years ago when I was writing an encyclopedia of positive Self-Talk, a good friend of mine sent me a set of self-talk "affirmation tapes." The tapes had been recorded by a gentleman who was obviously a fine and dedicated, spiritual individual. His tapes spoke at length of "wholeness" and "oneness with the great universal truth which exists within us."

I listened to those tapes for several hours. I listened to every word and thought. I even agreed with the principles which inspired them. But I did not hear one word of direction which would tell my subconscious mind *what to do about anything*. I do not fault the organizations and the faiths which teach those marvelously wonderful ideals for our minds to clutch and hold on to. The people of those faiths are some of the best Self-Talkers on this planet.

But if you want your life to change, get specific! If you are a supporter of the power of "affirmations," keep your motives high, but let your feet step down to touch the earth we are standing on.

Those of us whose dream it is to improve our lives, even in some small way, can do so. If you want to solve a problem (meet a challenge) or reach any goal, learn to give yourself the most precise and complete directions you can muster. If you have a problem, tackle it—but in the process, have a conversation with yourself. If you have a goal, no matter what it is, give yourself detailed instructions that tell you exactly what you want. And then stand back and get out of the way. Your expectations are about to happen.

CHAPTER NINETEEN

Internal Motivation

THERE IS AN energy which can create either motion or immobility in our lives. It is an energy which comes to us in the form of love, fear, joy, anger, passion, or despair. It comes to us as ecstacy, concern, pride, jealousy, desire, grief, compassion, or elation. These are our emotions; these are our motivators and our demotivators. They set us in motion—or they stop us in our tracks. They are the fires which infuse our lives with action, or burn us out in the smoldering embers of submission.

Earlier I gave you the example of managers who attempt to change the employee's attitude by using the "carrot or stick" method. I pointed out that using this method does not change attitudes. What it does do is to use natural emotions such as desire or fear, which are already within us, to temporarily motivate the individual into action.

How do we corral our emotional motivators to work for us? How do we pull the best out of ourselves and others—and help put the best into practice? In a previous chapter we discussed popular motivation techniques using outside motivation. Now let's get down to the specifics of how to use Self-Talk to motivate yourself.

The most common form of motivation is the *external* kind, when we rely on something outside of us to pat us on the back, nudge us, persuade us, or kick us in the behind to get us to go ahead and do what we already knew we should be doing in the first place.

External motivation does not necessarily come from a supportive friend who encourages you to do your best. Many of our external motivators aren't even human—and when it comes right down to it, they really don't care whether we make it or not.

To illustrate the point, let me give you a few examples of external motivators which do more than guide and direct us. These are the motivators that demand our attention and they insist on our most appropriate response: the boss, the bank loan, the mortgage payment, the dinner next Friday we agreed to go to but didn't want to attend, the orthodontist, the pile of unfinished paperwork on the desk, a mid-term exam, a favorite television program, the utility bill, or the ball game on Saturday.

Whether at first glance they appear to be or not, these are all motivators. And most of them could be called positive motivators. After all, they get us to pay the rent, get to work on time, keep up with our social requirements, take care of the family, and even give us some free time for ourselves.

THE POSITIVE PUSH

The best motivators, of course, the ones we like the most, are the motivators which get us to extend ourselves, achieve a little more, reach our goals, and live a better life. These usually come by way of someone telling us that we are capable of many great things, that we can conquer any obstacle or reach any goal. Motivational speakers are especially good at saying that sort of thing. But as much as we might enjoy being told how terrific we are by someone else, every form of external motivation is short-lived, no matter how demanding, exciting, or encouraging it might be.

What all of this amounts to is that all of us have a lot of motivations and a lot of motivators. The question is: Who is in control? Are you taking the responsibility for keeping yourself up and going or are you letting the circumstances of daily living assume the responsibility for you? Are you carefully deciding what motivates you and what does not? And most important of all, are you being motivated by outside influences or are you yourself the single most motivating factor in your own life?

If you would like to be in control of the forces in your life which influence and affect everything you do, then you most certainly would like to be in control of your own motivation. That would imply that you would like to motivate yourself in the best possible way—a way in which you can give yourself the strong, attention-getting, consistent, reliable, and effective motivation you need. That kind of motivation you will never get from anyone but yourself.

The only kind of motivation which we can ever be sure of is the motivation that is created within us—"internal" motivation. It is the kind of motivation which does not require the aid of anyone else—any assistance or support with someone or something else doing the real motivating for us. Self-motivation is the motivation which comes from having a sense of purpose, a sense of self-esteem and self-determination.

SOMETHING EVERYONE NEEDS

It doesn't make any difference what we do for a living or what we are doing in our lives right now; all of us need motivation. Whether you are a salesperson, athlete, manager or employee, the amount of motivation you have can make the difference between reaching your goals or falling short. Your motivation affects your position, your income, your determination, and your results. Like your attitude, your motivation affects everything you do.

Even if you are not in a competitive field, you still need motivation to keep you up and keep you going. I've known parents who have run out of motivation. When it came to raising their families, they ran out of steam. A motivated clergyman inspires more of his congregation than does a clergyman who has lost his inspiration himself. A student who is highly motivated to get good grades will spend more time studying than a student who is motivated only to get by.

All of us need motivation of one kind or another from the moment we arise in the morning to the moment we nod off to sleep at night. In fact, it could safely be said that the only time we do *not* need to be motivated is when we are sleeping, resting but going nowhere. The problem is that most of us learn to rely on external motivation when we should be learning self-reliance instead. People who are the most successful at whatever they do are those who are their own best motivators. They stand on their own feet, walk in the direction of their own choosing, and put themselves in charge of their own successes.

To motivate someone, anyone, to do anything, you must influence his *emotions!* In fact, there are many motivational psychologists who believe that you can never really motivate anyone else to do something they will not internally agree to do. Since our emotions are our motivators, the emotion must be changed or redirected before the motivation can take place. The same is true of motivating yourself.

Instead of relying on *any* outside source to help us motivate ourselves, think how much better it would be if we could always rely on ourselves for that same motivation. If we learn the right words to use when we talk to ourselves, we can easily learn to give ourselves the motivation we need, any time we need it.

This first example of Self-Talk for self-motivation is the kind of Self-Talk that is designed to get us emotionally "up." It talks to you *about you* in a way that gets you moving, while it supports that motivation with Self-Talk that gives you extra belief in yourself. You are not only programming yourself to meet the challenge, you are also giving yourself the extra insurance of the added belief that you can and will accomplish the task you are setting out to do.

This is Self-Talk that anyone can use at any time. It is not specific to any one area of self-motivation— making more sales, getting up on time, scoring points in a basketball game, or getting caught up on your paperwork—but it will work for all of these and more. This is Self-Talk that will give your subconscious mind a new set of directions which will help you motivate yourself in any area of your life:

I can do anything I believe I can do! I've got it and every day I get more of it. I have talent, skills, and ability.

I set goals and I reach them. I know what I want out of life. I go after it and I get it.

People like me, and I feel good about myself. I have a sense of pride in who I am and I believe in myself.

Nothing seems to stop me. I have a lot of determination. I turn problems into advantages. I find possibilities in things that other people never give a chance.

I have a lot of energy—I am very alive! I enjoy life and I can tell it and so can others. I keep myself up, looking ahead, and liking it.

I know that I can accomplish anything I choose, and I refuse to let anything negative hold me back or stand in my way.

I am not afraid of anything or anyone. I have strength, power, conviction, and confidence! I like challenges and I meet them head on, face to face—today especially!

I am on top of the world and I'm going for it. I have a clear picture in my mind of what I want. I can see it in front of me. I know what I want and I know how to get it. I know that it's all up to me and I know I can do it.

Roadblocks don't bother me. They just mean that I am alive and running, and I'm not going to stand still for anything.

I trust myself. I've got what it takes—plenty of it— and I know how to use it. Today, more than ever. Today I am unstoppable! *I've got myself together and I'm getting more together every day. And today—look out world, here I come!*

Limitations? I don't even recognize them as limitations. There is no challenge I can't conquer; there is no wall I can't climb over. There is no problem I can't defeat or turn around and make it work for me.

I stand tall! I am honest and sincere. I like to deal with people and they like me. I think well; I think clearly. I am organized; I am in control of myself, and everything about me.

I call my shots and no one has to call them for me. I never blame anyone else for the circumstances of my life. I accept my failings and move past them as easily as I accept the rewards for my victories.

I never demand perfection of myself, but I expect the very best of what I have to give—and that's what I get!

I never give myself excuses. I get things done on time and in the right way. Today I have the inner strength to do more than ever.

I am an exceptional human being. My goals and

my incredible belief in myself turn my goals into reality. I have the power to live my dreams. I believe in them like I believe in myself. And that belief is so strong that there is nothing that diminishes my undefeatable spirit.

Try reading *that* to yourself in front of the mirror each morning for the next few days! Wouldn't it be wonderful if we had someone who believed in us so much that every day we could count on being told those incredible, motivating truths about ourselves? If we had that, we would certainly have the truest and best friend we could ever find.

The truth is, of course, we *do* have that friend. Each of us does. Right up here inside ourselves. All we have to do is ask and our friend will be there, without fail, any time, in any circumstance.

GIVING LIFE TO YOUR SELF-TALK

When you first read these new words of self-belief and self-motivation, they can lie there on the page, looking like not much more than quietly reassuring inspirational thoughts. Bring them to life. Pull them off the page. Shout them out to yourself if you have to, but grab them, hold on to them, and make them your own.

If you are by yourself, stop for a moment, turn back a page or two and reread those same words, this time out loud. Give yourself permission to suspend your disbelief. Set your doubts aside. For just a few moments, speak to yourself as though you were the single most important person in the whole world. (You *are*, you know.)

Don't worry if at first you feel strange or uncomfortable talking to yourself in a new way. Unless you are already a practiced Self-Talker, it *should* feel a little strange. After all, you are giving your old programming quite a shock! It is probably not used to hearing a nonstop description of an incredible new you.

The more you do that, the easier and the more natural it will become. In not too long, even though your old programming may try to fight you for a time—it may even try to make you feel foolish and get you to stop—if you keep doing it, the new words will win out.

If while you are reading this you cannot privately say the new commands to yourself out loud, go back and reread the Self-Talk silently—this time word for word. Tell yourself to listen. Look at the pictures in your mind that see yourself actually being the individual you are describing to yourself.

Self-Talk is not just a few lines of encouraging words printed in the pages of a book. When you apply Self-Talk to *you*, those same words take life. The moment you begin to speak them or read them and consciously internalize them, they take on a personal meaning and life of their own—and they play a role that could become important to every part of your life. They *are* that best friend, that part of you which is telling you the truth about yourself.

If you're going to shock your subconscious with the new words, the new kind of Self-Talk, you might as well give it a full dose. Instead of ever letting the *de*motivators in your life weaken you or bring you to your knees, even for a moment, kick them out! Stand up, face them, point to the door and tell them to get out of your life. You're through with them, and you don't need them any longer. Stop them in *their* tracks! Overpower them.

Just when your subconscious thinks you're through, don't let up, give it some more. And this time start by making the conscious decision to *demand* that the internal you *listens very carefully:*

I know that greatness begins in the minds of the great. I know that what I believe about myself is what I will become—so I believe in the best for myself.

I am practical and realistic, and I keep my feet on solid ground. But I also give myself the freedom to live up to my fullest expectations.

I never limit myself by the short-sighted beliefs of others—instead I open myself up to the broad horizons of unlimited possibility.

When someone says I "cannot," I answer "why not?" When someone says "It's impossible," I answer that nothing is any more impossible than I believe it to be. And I truly believe that with my individual fortress of faith, with me, anything is possible.

I have drive, spirit, stamina, and endurance. I have a good strong winning attitude about myself and about everything I do. I am practical and realistic, but I also believe in the best possible outcome of any situation.

If I have ever had any doubts about myself in the past, today is a good day to put them aside. It's a good day to throw out any disbelief that ever held me back.

I know that I am headed in the right winning direction, and I look forward and never look back. I have the ability to focus on one thing at a time, so I concentrate my attention on the job at hand— and I get it done!

Today is one of those days when nothing can stand in my way. When I need extra determination, I've got it! When I need more energy and drive, I've got it! I've got the power to get it done and the patience to see it through, no matter what the job or challenge may be.

Right now, even while I am telling myself these truths about me, I know that I can succeed and I am succeeding. At this moment, if I think of any challenge in front of me, I know that I will become even more a winner because of it.

I keep my chin up, my head held high. I look, act, sound, think, and feel like the winner I am! Anytime a problem starts to get me down, I get myself right back up! I tackle problems and I solve them. When frustration or defeat threatens me, I just become that much stronger, more positive, better organized, and more determined than ever!

Right now, today, this very moment, I am capable of giving myself the gift of absolute self-assurance, self-belief, and powerful non-stop confidence in myself.

No matter what it is that requires the very best of me, I can do it and I know I can.

Today is a great day. And I've got what it takes. So I choose to do it right, do it well! I choose to live today with joy and love.

I know it's all up to me. One hundred percent!— every bit of it. All of it is in how I look at it and what I do about it! That's what winning is. That's why I am a winner.

I set my sights. I keep my balance. I don't hesitate. I don't hold back! I know that the world is full of opportunities. Look at what I can do; look at where I can go! Look at what I can do just by saying "Yes!" to myself!

Just look at what I can do today! I am incredible . . . and today is a great day to show it!

It is easy to see how that kind of self-direction can be reworded to apply specifically to any part of your life that needs to be motivated.

Olympic athletes use Self-Talk to motivate themselves to gold-medal performances; even some high school and professional athletes use Self-Talk in exactly the same way and with the same winning results. The words change but the message—and the internal motivation it creates—is the same. We still need the team captain and the coach, but with the right kind of Self-Talk, we make their jobs, and the winning achievements we create, a whole lot easier.

I doubt that I could find a single coach who would not jump at the chance to have an entire team of self-motivated Self-Talkers. Dozens of sports organizations already use Self-Talk techniques. When used correctly, the result is the kind of superior performance that creates a winning team.

GETTING UP
WHEN THINGS GET DOWN

Another example of a profession which has already begun to adopt the concepts of Self-Talk for Internal Motivation is the sales field. I mentioned earlier that salespeople need to maintain a constant attitude of self-belief because of the number of times they are turned down; everytime the competition wins, someone else loses. In the mind of the salesperson who lost the sale, that loss represents a failure. Because of this, the field of sales creates the largest demand for skilled, professional motivators.

I recommend that those organizations which rely on salespeople to present and sell their products or services, add Self-Talk training to their existing training programs. It is an easy step to take, but its effects can be profound.

Although you may not be in the management or occupation of selling, you probably know that each of us relies on "selling"—ourselves or our ideas—nearly every day of our adult lives. If you are in a management or sales position, read this next example of Self-Talk carefully. But even if you are not in the field of professional sales, notice how much of the Self-Talk for selling applies equally as well to the times in your life when you want to influence or persuade someone else to your way of thinking or to do something that *you* want to do.

There are twelve individual areas of selling, each of which has its own set of Self-Talk. They include such subjects as Prospecting, Making the Presentation. Overcoming Objections Internally, Follow-Through. and Keeping Yourself Up When the Chips are Down. For this example, however, I will combine the various areas and show you just a few samples which are representative of the Self-Talk for "selling":

I begin each day with a clear mind and a specific plan to get the most from my time and my effort. I follow my plan and I reach my goals.

An accurate description of me would include the words professional, hard-working, qualified, skillful, energetic, enthusiastic, organized, determined, and highly successful.

I am good at persuading others to my point of view. That is because I first and always recognize and understand the point of view of the individual to whom I am presenting my ideas, my product. or my service.

I know how to listen—and I do. I have learned to hear not only the words which are being said, but I also listen to the unspoken thoughts which lie behind them.

I am always prepared. I take the time to do it right. In everything I do, I am prepared, confident, self-assured, and successful.

I always take care of the details in my work. I enjoy the details of selling and I always tend to them on time and with full attention.

I keep myself "up." I know that making good sales presentations means keeping myself up, energetic, and in control. That is exactly the way I am, and my sales presentations are always professional and effective.

I never avoid confronting a problem or making a sales call of any kind. I keep myself working and that keeps me winning.

I deserve to make the sales I create. I know that success in selling starts with seeing myself as the capable, productive individual that I am.

I am always sincere and honest. I believe that all achievement in selling begins with trust, skill, and determination. I ask for the order frequently and without hesitation. At every "buying signal," I ask for the order—and I close!

Being told "no" never bothers me. Instead, hearing the word "no" doubles my determination and adds to my positive enthusiasm.

Given the technical skills to match, the salesperson who mentally "becomes" the individual we have just described, even in those few short self-directives, would undoubtedly rank high on the list of sales achievers for any sales organization. Having worked with many salespeople in the past, I have all too often heard quite the opposite kinds of self-talk.

Because of our own past programming, it is all too easy to slip into using the old self-talk demotivators of complaints, excuses, and doubts—all the reasons necessary to place the blame for failure and underachievement on someone or something else: the sales manager, the company, the commission structure, or the competition.

Instead of igniting the spark of self-belief, too many salespeople, just like many of us in our own careers, solve the day's problems by avoiding the action we know we should take. Instead of spending a few minutes engaged in the highly productive activity of motivating ourselves to take action, we engage ourselves in talking ourselves *out* of action, and into having another cup of coffee.

THE LIGHT THAT NEVER FAILS

We can learn to motivate ourselves. We can learn to become self-starters, doers, and achievers. To do that takes less time and less training than any other kind of motivational development I have ever encountered. We need only to begin, and our inner selves, the part of us that *wants* to achieve, will soon begin to follow the new lead which we are giving it.

There is a vital part of each of us that is anxiously waiting for us to tell it that "it's okay to go ahead and achieve." That's what it wanted to do all along. All it needed was a few new words.

There is a sleeping giant within us. It seeks and needs *the light that never fails*—the motivation that comes from us. If we feed it, each day, in just the right way, it will become a part of us which will conquer our fears, slay the dragons, and carry us on to our victories. It is a magical genie of untold powers, impatiently waiting for its release. It is the essential, self-fulfilling part of each of us. It has been waiting a long time for us to tell it what to do. Go ahead, indulge yourself! Give yourself an exciting treat. Let the giant loose. Tomorrow morning, wake it up.

CHAPTER TWENTY

Situational Self-Talk

THIS CHAPTER CONTAINS one of the simplest and yet most effective techniques for self-help for everyday life that I have ever encountered. In fact, it is perhaps because this technique is so disarmingly simple that it easily escapes our notice. It is a method which any of us can put into practice by the simple decision to do so. It is not a technique which must be studied to be learned; to do it, you only have to be aware of it—and do it. And while the more you practice it the better it works, it will also work for you the first time you use it.

I have to admit that when I first explored the use of "Situational" Self-Talk, I could not help but wonder if it could be possible that something so obvious, so simple, could work so well. I was well aware from studying and observing many different self-help techniques, however, that the most effective techniques were always the simplest and most obvious. That description also fits Situational Self-Talk.

If this form of Self-Talk seems too uncomplicated to be valuable, I urge you to try it for yourself. Try it for a day, then for a week, and then for three or four. By then you will have the habit of using Situational Self-Talk automatically and it will no longer seem unimportant or ridiculously simple to you. It will become one of your strongest allies in your own personal growth and success. What is this simple key that is claimed to unlock such great treasure?

MAKING AN INSTANT ADJUSTMENT

A friend of mine related the story of her aunt, who for many years, although she did not like to cook, had to do so in order to take care of her large and growing family. Each time the aunt went into the kitchen to begin preparing a meal, she would say to herself, out loud, "This is going to be fun. I'm going to have a good time cooking today."

Later, after the meal was over and the dishes were done, she would say, "That wasn't so bad!"—and it wasn't. By giving herself a few simple words of Self-Talk she changed a chore into an acceptable task. She didn't change the work itself but she changed how she felt about it.

That is "Situational Self-Talk." *It is the kind of Self-Talk that adjusts situations by adjusting how we look at them*. It is a practical, immediate, *now* kind of Self-Talk that you can call on at any time and will come to your aid the moment you use it. Situational Self-Talk differs from the kinds of Self-Talk we have talked about in the last few chapters in that it does not require a "script" of Self-Talk to create a result. It can be accomplished in a moment, out loud or silently to yourself. It can be a single thought, or it can be a few well-chosen words.

Situational Self-Talk also differs from the other forms of positive Self-Talk in that it does not have to be phrased in the "present tense" only. It is already dealing with the here and now, today, or the near future. Its first objective is not to try to create a new, long-term internal picture of yourself; its primary job is to deal with today, *today*. So when you say to yourself, "I'm going to enjoy going to work today," the words you are using are *future* tense (going to), but they are still dealing with *now*.

Like the other kinds of Self-Talk, this "instant" form may help your attitude, overpower a bad habit, help you solve a problem or reach a goal, or motivate you to do better, but it accomplishes the task in a different way.

Situational Self-Talk is used when you are confronted with any situation which you would rather not be in, or when you are presented with an unexpected opportunity which requires your immediate attention. In most cases, this kind of Self-Talk is used to overcome some momentary circumstance which disagrees with you. I'll give you an example.

You are at work and the phone rings. It is a call from someone who you have been putting off talking to, and you know you need to take the call. You don't want to, but you know the problem has to be met with sooner or later. You have the choice of talking to the person or putting the confrontation off until another time. By then, the problem probably will have gotten worse. What you do next is your choice; the decision to take the call or put it off is entirely up to you.

It is at a time like this when just a few words of the right kind of Self-Talk can help you do the right thing. Instead of saying to yourself, "Oh, no, not him again! Tell him I'll call him back," you can use Self-Talk to tackle the problem then and there:

I like solving problems. I always deal with problems and I never avoid them. I'll take the call and I'll tackle the problem head on.

In this instance it takes about five or six seconds to give yourself these few words of Self-Talk. And in doing so you may save yourself hours of future grief. Taking the time to consciously convince yourself to do the right thing has not only saved you time, it has done something else which is far more important to you in another way: it has created a minor success in the development of your personal credibility—a small but important gold star on your report card of self-esteem.

I am often convinced that Situational Self-Talk, this seemingly simplest form of Self-Talk, is at times the most valuable of all. If you are consciously practicing the other forms of Self-Talk for getting your life together and working at improving yourself in other important ways, using Situational Self-Talk becomes an almost automatic by-product of the other Self-Talk you are using. But unless you are aware of this special kind of Self-Talk, you may not recognize how easy it is to use and how much good it can do for you.

DRIVING YOURSELF
TO DISTRACTION

A few years ago I fit into the category of individuals who give themselves minor emotional fits when they are driving in traffic. I know people who verbalize near-obscenities (or worse) at traffic lights which change at the wrong time or at other drivers who do wrong things like pulling in front of them or cutting them off. When they were about to be late they hit, with equal force, the brake, the gas pedal, and the horn.

It doesn't seem to have a lot to do with how important it is that they didn't get started on time. Behind the steering wheel all vengeance is meted out with equal fury. After this emotional driving style becomes a habit, these otherwise fine individuals get so used to driving with stress that they clutch the steering wheel with the same Indianapolis 500 grip when they aren't late for anything or when they are going nowhere in particular.

A friend of mine, the owner of a successful business in the Los Angeles area, is, in his normal waking state, one of the coolest, most staid individuals I have ever met. He is always kind, considerate, deferent, and understanding—except when he is trying to cross lanes on the Los Angeles freeway and someone unwittingly pulls his vehicle in front of him.

My basic belief in the goodness of humanity tells me that the young man driving the second-hand car who pulls into the wrong position in front of my friend's late-model foreign import on the freeway is probably an okay person. If he only knew what adjectives had just been expleted on his behalf! And then, moments later, my friend is once again his cool, calm, caring and collected self. That is, until the next unfortunate soul steers his car in the wrong direction, and my friend once again unleashes a torrent of temper on the unsuspecting driver of the other vehicle.

My own particular automotive stress-builders were stoplights and slow-moving traffic. One day, while driving to my office, I found myself anxiously anticipating the change in every traffic light I encountered between my home and my office. Halfway there I came to the astounding realization that I was doing my attitude, and probably my health, a great injustice. More than that, I realized that my behavior was not that which should be expected of a mature adult. I was dealing with traffic at about the same level that an eighteen-month-old child deals with hunger.

I made an instant decision. I decided that never again would traffic, in any situation, cause me stress. I reinforced my decision with a few simple lines of Situational Self-Talk:

I enjoy relaxing while I am driving in the car.

I always give myself the necessary amount of time to get anywhere I am going. I always arrive at—or before—the time I need to be there.

Traffic lights change at their own discretion: not mine. If the light changes before I get there, I will stop, wait for the light to change, and relax while I am waiting.

Slow-moving or standing traffic is not a problem to me. I now enjoy the time I have to organize my thoughts and think about those things which are beneficial to me. I will get there when I get there.

The self-suggestions took hold. A few times since then, on the way to an airport, a little behind schedule, I have had to consciously restate my Self-Talk. But since that day I have felt differently when I drive. Was it a difficult change to make? No. Could anyone else do the same? Yes.

THE CHEMICALS OF STRESS

What aggravation we give ourselves! What emotions we force ourselves to endure. Mind/brain researchers have gained great insight into the process of the effect of the *natural* chemicals our brains trigger and dump into our systems—just from a minute or two of negative emotional stress.

A few minutes of anger, anxiety, negative stress, and frustration can literally toxify our physical systems for hours. Why do we do it? Why do we let ourselves get out of control? We do it because we thought it was okay to be that way; we grew up not quite shaking off the last vestiges of immaturity.

We kept a few of the negative behavior styles of our childhood with us so we could trot them back out when things don't go the way we'd like them to go.

In businesses I have seen some usually level-headed people, from the Chairman of the Board to the first-time secretary, momentarily throw their sanities out the window because life, at that moment, wasn't the way they wanted it to be.

We are all very human. But there is nothing stopping us from stepping past a human frailty or two and rising above the crowd. If people around you choose to let situations and circumstances control them, there probably is not too much you can do about it. But you *can* do something about yourself—how you deal with every situation you confront, every unexpected jack-in-the-box complication, and every circumstance in your life which you cannot change or control.

All of us have dozens of things we would like to change—in our jobs, in our personal lives, at home, at school, with our friends, with the rules and laws we live by, with those who govern us, with how we spend our time—with everything about us.

CONSCIOUS ACTIONS OR UNCONTROLLED REACTIONS

But how we react to those things in life which we can do nothing about will always be the truest test of our own self-control, our own individual sense of self, and our ability to manage our minds and ourselves in a way that keeps us coming out on top and at peace with where we are. That is a part of maturity. That is taking responsibility for ourselves and living it, every day.

I am frequently amazed at the number of people who consistently complain about things they can do nothing about. How often we hear someone complain about something as totally uncontrollable as the *weather!* We have all known someone who let rain or an overcast sky ruin an entire day. The weather does exactly what it wants to do; the loudest complaint won't change it. Complaining about anything out of our control is not only senseless, but the negative self-talk we use to lodge the complaint has a direct effect on how we function that day—mentally *and* physically!

It is so much easier and healthier to recognize the reality of the situation as it actually is (such as weather) and adjust our own Self-Talk to accept it and possibly even enjoy it. Why not? It's going to rain anyway! Try looking at it differently. Give yourself a few words of Self-Talk that will direct your subconscious and conscious minds to see things differently, at least for that day:

> *It's raining today and that's fine with me. I'm going to have a good day and a little rain can't stop me.*

There is an increasing amount of medical and scientific evidence which tells us that something as simple as "having a good attitude" is much more than just a good idea.

We've known for years that having a good frame of mind made things work better for us. But we now know that something as incidental as having the right "frame of mind" plays a part in a mental and biological chain reaction that involves every facet of *what* we are and *who* we are—every moment, throughout our entire lives.

Research in the field of neuroscience suggests that such things as thoughts, moods, attitudes, and actions play a far more important role in our mental and physical chemistry than we had ever thought possible. To us, the beneficiaries of this field of scientific research, the conclusions can be startling. How important are a few casual thoughts? They are more important than we had ever imagined.

Our biological environment, our physical makeup and health, affects our state of mind. The better condition our internal biological environment is in, the better we think and act. The reverse is also true. The more productively we think, the more positively we affect ourselves emotionally and physically.

THE SITUATION CYCLE

Just the simple act of telling yourself you are going to have a "good day," as an example, not only helps convince you mentally, it sets off chemical/electrical triggers in your brain which affect your mental state, which in turn affects you physiologically, which in turn affects how you think.

It is a self-generating cycle: thought, emotional response, physiological response, thought, emotional response, and so on, until something breaks or changes the cycle. That is why one negative incident, first thing in the morning, can cause a chain reaction which, if left unchecked, can affect everything else throughout the day. It affects our energy and our enthusiasm, our initiative and our spirit.

The implication of this is that you can successfully scuttle an entire day by allowing even a single event to create the first step in a negative cycle. This negative cycle is not caused by the problem or event that appears to set it off—the cycle begins with how you *respond* to the problem in the first place.

That is why it's just not practical, physiologically or mentally, to complain or get "down" about normal daily irritations—or any of the things you can do nothing about. But you *can*, instead, within moments, change how you feel about them. Instead of creating a *negative* cycle, you can create a *positive* cycle anytime you choose. For most of us, creating positive cycles is a far more enjoyable way to make it through the day.

Of course, we've all met those individuals who seem to enjoy being miserable. No matter how well things are going for them they will find something to help them feel unhappy. Fortunately, most of us like to feel good. We would rather be happy than unhappy—we would rather feel good than feel bad. And the truth is anyone can feel happy or unhappy, in tune or out of control, almost anytime they want to. Your own internal Self-Talk is not a magic solution for every situation that comes up, but it can help you stay in control and deal with each of them more realistically and more effectively.

We should not expect ourselves to have a smile on our faces every moment of the day. But I suspect that all of us would fare better at life by working at smiling a little more—maybe a lot more.

MAKING THE *BEST* OF *LESS*-THAN-THE-BEST

There are times, however, when we are faced with situations which are quite normal, but which do not call for a countenance of eternal bliss. If you have ever taken a child into the emergency room at eleven o'clock at night, and left an hour later with your child sixteen stitches stronger and your bank account two hundred and fifty dollars poorer, you know what I mean.

If that happened to you, imagine what would be going on in your mind. Even if the injury were not serious, you would be concerned. When the child came running in with the injury, whatever you were doing would have been immediately interrupted and you would probably spend the next hour or two sitting in the waiting area at the emergency room. It would not be the perfect ending to a beautiful day.

If that situation happened to you, how would you feel? What unconscious thoughts would you say to yourself? More than likely your emotions would be running somewhere between anger, concern, and being just plain upset!

What you say to yourself at a time like that will affect the frame of mind you are in, how you feel, and how well you handle the situation—and yourself. How well your son or daughter does will depend on the doctor and whatever words of encouragement you can offer. How well *you* do is entirely up to you! If you have made the decision to be in control of yourself, you will talk to yourself in the right way—immediately, directly, realistically, and positively.

Situational Self-Talk doesn't expect you to instantly change every bad situation into a good situation. It simply gives you a way to consciously put the best construction on any situation. It keeps you in control—of yourself—and allows you to function at your best under any circumstance that comes along.

Have you ever been driving alone when you had a

flat tire? I would wager that the self-talk that happens next is usually less than the best kind.

If you have a spare, and can change the tire your-self, you pull over, get out, open the trunk, wrestle the spare to the ground, find the jack and fight it out of its hiding place, jack up the car, force the hubcap from its locked-in position, physically and verbally fight the nuts off the wheel lugs, jockey the spare onto the hub, replace the nuts, pound the hubcap back into place, get back into the car and continue on your way.

As you drive off you do your best to rub the dirt smudges from your pants, dress, or suitcoat; by coin-cidence you were not wearing your tire-changing clothes when the incident happened.

The Self-Talk that goes on from the moment we have the flat tire, to some time after, perhaps long after, either keeps us in control and keeps our spirits up; or as happens in most circumstances like this, our own words, our own thoughts, make the problem worse.

All too often, the words we have said to ourselves when things went wrong *contributed* to the problem—instead of making it better or helping us solve it. If you think about it, have you ever seen anyone whistling, humming a happy tune, or smiling while he was chang-ing a flat tire on the side of the road?

ENDLESS OPPORTUNITIES TO BREAK OR *MAKE* YOUR DAY

Things that get us upset can be anything and every-thing. Each day we are confronted with an obstacle course of endless possibilities of things which could upset us, make us angry, or drive us to distraction—if we let them. The daily events that occur in the lives of even a few of us would give us an almost endless list of daily frustrations. The results of just one or two of them happening to you can create, with the wrong kind of self-talk, reason enough to get thrown off course. If the frustration is big enough it can ruin the whole day.

Situational Self-Talk may not change the problem, but if used consciously and immediately, the moment the need arises, it can rapidly change how you respond to the problem at hand and how you do for the rest of the day. Some of these situations are important, but some of them can be so petty that it's hard to see how they could upset us at all. What they all have in common is the way we react to them.

They are the causes of arguments, frustrations, anxiety, stress, and bad days—and they can be anything at all, large or small: the toast is burned; the plane is late; the boss is giving you a hard time; one of the kids came home with a bad report card; you're halfway through your shower and you run out of hot water; your favorite television program got preempted; you're late for work and you can't find anything to wear; your promotion didn't come through; etc., etc., etc. Are the things that go wrong all that bad? To our subconscious minds, they are exactly as bad as we perceive them to be—as we tell ourselves that they are.

Instead of getting needlessly upset (and thereby starting a negative cycle) when you have to stand and wait in line, practice saying something different to yourself. Instead of thinking "I hate standing in line," it is just as easy to use some Self-Talk to change how you look at standing in lines. If you wonder if it works, try it the next chance you get:

I don't mind standing in line. That's where I am and I'm doing what I need to do. Standing in line doesn't bother me—and I really like getting things done.

I know people who hate to get an answering-machine message when they are trying to reach someone on the telephone. "I hate answering machines" is the program they have convinced themselves to believe. Actually, answering machines aren't all that bad. They help a lot of people stay in touch when they can't be by the phone. They make it possible for people to do something else without leaving the phone completely unattended. They serve their purpose. We can either decide to let them upset us or we can recognize that they are a part of the technology of this century and decide to accept them; make them okay. The alternative is usually no one answering the phone.

Telling yourself that you don't like to talk to a recorded message won't stop people from using them. It can't, for the present, be changed. What you can change is how you respond to them: "I'm glad I have the chance to leave a message."

IT IS AS IT IS

Whatever the example, it doesn't matter whether we are in the camp of those who like the way the situation is or not. If it is a situation that *is*, then it *is!*

I know people who do not like to wear seat belts when they are driving or riding in a car. They can be heard to proclaim every possible reason why they should not have to wear them. The reasons range from how seat belts wrinkle their clothes or how uncomfortable they are, to saying that wearing them should be an individual choice, not a law. If, wherever it is that you drive, you have to wear them, then you have the choice of wearing them or not. But if you want to follow the rules, you have the choice of telling yourself what a nuisance you think they are or telling yourself that they don't bother you at all. They can be a daily grievance or they can be nothing more than a safety device that is there—and there is no need to give it a second, negative, thought.

Just as Situational Self-Talk will work for the smallest of inconveniences, it will work equally well in more important circumstances—those, as an example, which directly affect our income and our professional growth. When I work with corporations and businesses I hear grievances and resentments from individuals at every level of the corporate structure. Most of them are expressions of dissatisfaction with things that the individual can do nothing about. It may be company policy, government regulation, or a manager's actions—all of which are a part of normal business life.

The positive Self-Talker soon learns to recognize the unchangeable realities of business. He not only makes the best of them and stops fighting them—consciously and unconsciously—but gets busy helping the company move ahead so he can have a good place to work and an opportunity to further his career. After spending many years in business environments, I could fill several chapters of a book discussing techniques and methods to overcome the obstacles of personal attitudes and applying Self-Talk to productivity in our jobs and careers. Just imagine what making minor, daily attitude shifts could do for us on the job!

I have never tried to estimate the number of major and minor problems and upsets the average individual faces in a month or a year. There is no need to dwell on them; we all have enough of our own. I've used just a few examples to give you the idea. I am sure by now you have thought of your own examples. Think of anything in your day that gets in the way, and you'll find an opportunity that could use some Situational Self-Talk.

There are even times when others around us will use any persuasive techniques possible to get us thinking in the right direction. I remember the story of the rather clever bride who dented the fender of her husband's new sports car. The car was his pride and joy, and she knew that the smallest nick in the paint would be a calamity to him. When she arrived home she rushed into the house in hysterics, "I've just had the most horrible accident and I've wrecked your car!" The husband, who was instantly concerned for his wife's safety, was greatly relieved when she assured him, through her tears, that she had come out of the wreck unscathed.

Caught between his concern for his bride's well-being and agonizing over the loss of the car, the husband finally asked his wife where the car was now. "It's in the driveway," she said, still trying to calm herself down. The husband, worried and shaken, put his arm around his wife and together they walked out to the driveway to view the battered remains of his shiny new car. When he saw the small dent in the fender his worst fears turned to joyous elation. "It's nothing at all! I'm just glad you weren't hurt. We can get it fixed—look, it's just a small dent! It's hardly even noticeable!"

If the wife had instead walked into the house and announced, "I just put a dent in your new car," I am sure the husband's reaction would have been a little different. I suspect that his self-talk that evening would not have been thoughts of relief and thankfulness. In this instance, the new bride, who had obviously figured out her husband pretty well, set up his self-talk for him. Most of the time, however, we are not so well set up; we have to find our own self-talk and fend for ourselves.

If the husband had been a practiced, positive Self-Talker in the first place, his wife could have used a more direct approach to the problem. The important point is that our responses to situations are based on what we perceive—what we say to ourselves either consciously or unconsciously at the time. The dent in the fender, it turned out, was not the issue. The position the husband took, *internally,* was.

THE NEXT SITUATION IS A CHANCE TO RESPOND

The position each of us takes—internally—will always determine how we react, how we respond to any occurrence that confronts us. If being stalled in traffic sends your blood pressure off the chart, wouldn't it seem smart to put yourself back in control?

If, in the past, aggravations have become hindrances, you can stop them from continuing to get in your way. If you have allowed the "details of life," the natural occurrences of daily living to affect you negatively, upset you, get you off track, or ruin your day, you can change that, starting any time you like.

If each of us at the moment of birth were given a quart jar of energy, and if we could use it up any way we chose, do you suppose most of us would use our energy in a wholesome, worthwhile way? I'm sure we'd like to. If you could choose for yourself, right now, how you were going to use the energy you have left, how would you use it? Would you scatter it about on anger, complaints, and on the minor dissatisfactions of life? Or if you had only a limited amount, would you use it carefully, applying it to the thoughts and the tasks which would give you fulfillment and peace of mind?

The day each of us was born, we were given that energy—minute bits of electro-chemical energy which feed small but important messages to our minds. One day, when the energy jar is empty, those thoughts, combined together, will have created in our lives the sum total of every worthwhile thing we have done. Our thoughts are the gold coins in the treasure chest of our inheritance. Each one valuable by itself, they are the thoughts we are given to use any way we choose. When we recognize the incredible importance of every one of those small, energizing thoughts, why would we want to carelessly throw them away, use them up, without extracting the most we can get from each of them?

The next time a problem of any kind occurs, take note of how you respond to it. If you consider yourself to be a mature, capable individual, in control of yourself, *take control* of your thoughts. Not just when it suits you and not just when things go well. Don't waste the power of your mind giving in to the petty inconveniences of life. Use that energy for something good! Channel it, control it, focus it. Give yourself the words and directions that put you in control of yourself. It isn't difficult, and it's always worth it!

CHAPTER TWENTY-ONE

Getting Started

I HAVE FOUND THAT after learning about Self-Talk and understanding its use, people will fall into one of three general categories:

A. Those who actively pursue a plan of action to put the principles of Self-Talk to work. They address the possibilities of using their new form of Self-Talk with dedication and anticipation. They make it a conscious and active part of their goals and achievement path.

B. Those who accept the basic principles of Self-Talk and adapt those principles into their lives in a casual, non-specific way. They apply the concepts of Self-Talk but they do not actively work at developing them; rather they simply apply them as they see fit and allow them to work.

C. Those who do nothing about it and gain nothing from it.

If you are in one of the first two categories, I will offer some suggestions which will help you get the most from the Self-Talk principles we have discussed. It is one thing to learn *about* something; it is quite another thing to put something that is learned into practice.

Let us say that there is a part of your mind which wants you to move forward, to get ahead—both in your external world and inside yourself. If that is the case, there are several things you can do to begin putting Self-Talk into practice beginning now. Most of the steps are easy to do. Some will take a little more work. Whether you do any of them or all of them, you will benefit from the effort.

A FEW PRACTICAL STEPS

We discussed earlier that if something (in self-development) is not simple, it will not work. I will make the steps as simple and as practical as possible. No one expects you to move mountains in a day, but no one who cares about you at all would expect you to sit still and do nothing. So I will suggest some steps that you can take.

If you do not follow any of them your results will be minor. If you give them your best efforts, and add some of the personal enthusiasm and determination which I know you have, you will create in your life new and exciting adventures. You will open doors, seek new opportunities, conquer new challenges, and achieve new rewards. You will accomplish things which few others ever dream of. You will do things that no one else can ever do for you.

If you have been a student of achievement, those words should sound familiar; they echo the promises of gurus and motivators. They offer you—if you will only follow their system and use their winning techniques—the motivation to succeed even if the motivation and the success is temporary. This is where learning to use Self-Talk makes a vital difference.

I'll give you some practical ideas and you can try them for yourself. But I will not offer you some ultimate system of success. *No one* can give you that. That you must give to yourself. I suggest only that you take back the control of your own personal mental computer. Take the keyboard back—program it for yourself, shape your life in the form of your own choosing, and accept the results with the secure knowledge of having done it for yourself.

When you begin to change the directions, the thoughts that you give to your own subconscious mind, you are putting yourself back in control! If you stay with it, you will become your own person. No one else will ever be able to take *you* away from you again.

THE EFFECTS OF SELF-DIRECTION

During the past several years, I have had the pleasure of knowing a number of individuals who learned the value of talking to themselves in the right way. They are astonishing people. Many of them came from humble beginnings, but their lives today are testimonials to the amazing effects of self-actualization.

They have become the most natural achievers I have ever met. Regardless of their career path or role in life, they stand apart. They don't have to talk about confidence, they radiate it. They don't have to exhibit their success, they live it. They don't pretend to care, they *care*. Each of them, in his or her own way, is playing a part in making the world a little better. I have often thought that if there were enough of them, all of us would be better off.

I have two sons, both grown. Both struggled and finessed their way into maturity in the same way the rest of us grew up—they were faced with similar heredities, environments and choices—the same determining factors which direct the futures of most of us. But of all the individuals that I know, they are two of the finest human beings I have met. I am not speaking of them with the pride of a parent; that we all do. But I have noticed there is something unusual about them.

I know them as uniquely astute, aware, caring individuals whom I would have liked to have known were they not related to me in any way. They speak their minds, stand their ground, and defend their honor to the end. They are the sort of people who add to the world by living in it. I have tried to figure out what it is that gives them a quality that I would like to have had when I was young. I can isolate only one thing. They learned how to talk to themselves.

I have watched the astonishing metamorphosis of an average individual, growing through a new awareness, into a bright, magnificent being. I have witnessed the cocoon of indifference give way to the wings of self-belief. I have been honored to know those individuals who developed such a mighty sense of *self* that they had enough left over to give away—and lived their lives giving to others. Some of them I have never met, but I know them. They are those who have conquered themselves. They have captured a part of the driving force within themselves and aimed it in the right direction; they have come to grips with truth. They are in touch with who they are.

They have purpose and understand their reason for being; they take counsel with themselves—and they listen to what they have to say. They are a part of the hope which dwells in each of us. They are the *true* achievers.

Are any of them so different from the rest of us? I don't think so. They have only made the minor change of putting their lives—and their "selves"—in order. They have won the battle of being in control of who they are and what they choose to do with their lives.

If you would like to make a difference, if you would like to be back in control—where you belonged in the first place—try some of the following. If it works for you, do more of it. If it doesn't work the first time, try it again. I have not yet been introduced to the person who cannot make it work. If you want it to—it will.

LISTEN TO YOUR OWN SELF-TALK

For the next forty-eight hours, listen to every word of self-talk that you say to yourself. Bad, good, or otherwise, listen to every word you say out loud or silently to yourself or about yourself. *Consciously* listen to every thought you think to yourself.

227

Listen for both kinds of self-talk—negative and positive. Notice especially the self-talk that creeps up unconsciously. If tomorrow morning the toast is burned, listen to what you say to yourself about it. If you have been thinking about doing something but haven't yet gotten it done, bring the subject up. See what response you get from the *inside* you.

Listen to the way you respond to problems and the way you react to opportunities. Watch your reaction to "risks." Is your old self-talk keeping you in the corners and shadows or are you standing up and standing tall? Does your self-talk say you are on top, confident, and going for it, or does it hold you back? Can you count yourself as basically "negative" or "positive"? And most important of all—and be honest about this—have you been a negative self-talker or a positive Self-Talker?

Listen to what you say when you talk to yourself. It is perfectly okay if for the next two days your friends think you look a little distracted. Just keep listening to yourself. What you hear will tell you a lot about what you're going to do about it.

LISTEN TO THE SELF-TALK OF OTHERS

During the same time, listen to the self-talk, the "self-speak" of others—especially the self-talk of your own family members, your close friends, and your associates at work. Listen to everything they say about themselves and about what they think and feel about anything they talk about. There is no faster way to convince yourself how anti-productive negative self-talk can be than watching other people put themselves through it.

For the time being, don't say anything to anyone else about their own self-talk—just observe. You'll have plenty of time to initiate someone else at a later time. Listen especially to what we call "opinions." All opinions reflect either our own beliefs or, when we have no opinion of our own, the beliefs of others. Notice how it influences someone's self-talk.

Also look for signs of who is in control in that person's life. Who is wielding the stick or the cushion—the boss, spouse, social image, money, security? A person's self-talk will always tell you, if you listen long enough, what their external motivations are.

Listen for something called "Social-talk." That is the self-talk that others (and sometimes we) use which places priorities on social importance—something like keeping up with the Joneses. Social-talk is very influential. It lets us know what we "ought" to do, whether it makes any sense or not.

MAKE A LIST OF YOUR OWN PAST SELF-TALK

This next step takes a little work, but if you spend even twenty or thirty minutes doing it, it should prove to be revealing to you. If you are starting this project with someone else (husband, wife, friend), you might be interested in sharing notes at the end of this step.

Write down, on a single sheet of paper, the ten most significant negative self-talk suggestions that you give yourself most often. Don't fudge and don't mind being personal. List those self-talk phrases you use most. If you can't think of ten of them you aren't trying. Most of us use several dozen self-talk phrases that we are not even aware of.

Remember, these are "negative" self-talk (Level I or Level II) phrases—things like, "I can't . . ." "Nothing seems to go right," or "It's just not my day." Those are only examples. There are hundreds to choose from.

Save your list of your ten "most-used" negative self-talk phrases. We'll come back to them later.

BECOME AWARE OF THE INFLUENCE OF "MEDIA-TALK"

For the next seven days, listen to what we call "Media-talk." That's the programming you are receiving from radio, television, the daily newspaper, magazines, etc. You will also hear an edited, and usually subjective, version of Media-talk when you listen to the self-talk of other people around you.

The important thing to remember while you are observing and collecting examples of Media-talk is how you respond to the Media-talk programming you are receiving. (Have you ever bought the brand of tissue you saw advertised the most on TV?)

The reason for this step is to acquaint you with something called "external influence." We all know what it means, but we seldom sit down and think about the effect it has in our lives. Have you ever considered how many things you do because you felt *obliged* to do them?

YOUR GREATEST RESPONSIBILITY

The more aware you become of all of the persuasions and conditioning which go on in your life, the easier it will be for you to recognize them for what they are and do something about them. It's a healthy idea to stop now and then and ask yourself the question, *"Who's in control here?"* Once aware of how programming works and where it comes from, who do you suppose is responsible for what is programmed into your own mind? You are, of course.

To some people, that is a burdensome responsibility. But think how freeing it can be! Creating your own thoughts and determining the direction of your own *future* is the most important personal responsibility you will ever have—and taking that responsibility will give you more control over your own life than you ever have had before.

Once you are aware of the self-talk around you, both from others and from yourself, it is only natural that you might want to take personal control over the self-talk in your future. The next step is to begin creating Self-Talk for yourself.

CHAPTER TWENTY-TWO

Creating Your Own Self-Talk

THE BEST WAY to begin practicing using Self-Talk is to create new Self-Talk for yourself. To show you how easy this can be, you might like to take a few minutes and write a short Self-Talk script on something very simple. Or you can do this exercise in your head.

When I wrote *The Complete Book of Self-Talk*, I addressed fifty-two specific areas of Self-Talk that related directly to daily life—at home, on the job, dealing with ourselves internally, dealing with other people in our lives, reaching goals, and personal growth. In that book I wrote out complete word-for-word Self-Talk scripts for each of those fifty-two areas of "daily living." The book was designed to be a ready reference manual for anyone who wanted to immediately begin using Self-Talk in literally any area of life—and have word-for-word Self-Talk instantly available—for job, home, family, goals, problems, and individual potential.

In writing that book, I researched, identified, collected, and carefully rewrote more than fourteen hundred Self-Talk phrases and self-suggestions. In the process I learned that there is no thought which, although it may have worked against us in the past, cannot be reworded into a self-direction which works for us. Our Self-Talk is never exclusive—it includes anything and everything we will ever think about. And any of it or all of it can be rephrased to work a little— or a lot—better for us.

THE RIGHT SELF-TALK
FOR EVERY SUBJECT

When you begin rephrasing your own Self-Talk you can choose any subject that comes to mind, and cover it with the right kind of Self-Talk. I'll give you some examples to help you get started.

Earlier I suggested that you make a list of ten phrases of negative self-talk which you have used in the past. It is sometimes surprising to learn how easy it is, with a little practice, to turn those phrases around. Any negative self-talk phrase you use can be turned into positive Self-Talk. In a short time you'll find that using them the right way is just as easy and will come just as naturally to you as using them the old way.

Let's take a few examples of the kind of self-talk phrases that we would find on a typical list of negative self-talk. These may not be the same examples that you have used for yourself, but the way you turn any of them around will work the same way as the examples we'll use. Here is a sample list of negative self-talk. These examples may not be the same comments you make to yourself, and they may not represent the same problems or opportunities you face, but they should be similar:

1. "Things aren't going very well for me at work."

2. "I just can't seem to communicate with my son anymore." (This could be anyone you feel you're having a hard time talking to.)

3. "I have a hard time getting out of bed in the morning."

4. "Today has been a tough day."

5. "I really need to get more exercise."

6. "I'd like to put more money into savings, but I just don't seem to be able to."

7. "I wish I had more time."

Think back to the Self-Talk "scripts" we discussed in the preceding chapters. If you have written out examples of your own negative self-talk you can now write them again, a different way—in the positive, and in most cases, in the *present* tense. If you haven't written a list, think about the examples of negative self-talk that come to mind and mentally do the same thing—reword them.

Example One:
The self-statement, **"Things aren't going very well for me at work,"** can easily be changed to, "*I enjoy my work. I understand the problems and I get past them.*"

Example Two:
Programming your subconscious with the self-de-

feating words, **"I just can't seem to communicate with my son anymore,"** can just as easily be rephrased into a new self-program: *"I take the time to listen, talk, and communciate. I'm patient and understanding. It's worth working at, and I do."*

Example Three:

Telling yourself that you **"have a hard time getting out of bed in the morning,"** certainly won't help you get out of bed any faster or easier. *Every time* the thought comes up, change the words to, *"It's easy for me to get out of bed in the morning. I get up and I get at it!"* Repeat that to yourself for a few days—or for as long as it takes. Eventually you will override the old program that made it tough for you to get up in the first place.

Keep in mind that changing just one or two phrases isn't going to make a sweeping change in your life. If you want to make some changes, change as *many* of the old phrases as you can find. The more of the old self-talk you change, and the more often you use the new Self-Talk when you talk to yourself about the subject, the better you'll do at making the change and making it permanent.

Example Four:

Instead of ever again telling yourself **"Today has been a tough day,"** think about what that tells your subconscious. If you are telling yourself that just because it was a difficult day it must have been a *bad* day, it can only make you feel less than successful—that day! And all that does is convince your subconscious mind that you have failed.

Repeating anything that implies to your subconscious that you have failed will only convince it that failing is a pattern it should create! You don't have to pretend that the day was wonderful, but it isn't necessary to convince yourself that the day was a disaster, either. You worked hard and not everything worked out the way you wanted it to. Give yourself a break. Reshape the thought: *"Today was fine. I feel good about myself. And tomorrow will be even better!"* That's not ignoring the problems or the hard work. It's simply putting *you* back on top.

Example Five:

If you would really like to get yourself in better physical shape, but haven't gotten around to doing something about it, telling yourself **"I really need to get more exercise,"** will only help you put it off. I like the Self-Talk phrase, *"I exercise every day."* I would add a few supporting phrases like, *"I enjoy exercising and I really like how it makes me feel. I like keeping myself in shape mentally and physically. I look good and I feel good; and daily exercise keeps me that way. I look forward each day to exercising my body, exercising my mind, and keeping myself fit and winning."*

Example Six:

"I'd like to put more money into savings but I just don't seem to be able to," is the kind of "money" self-talk that many of us have used. Using it doesn't help a bit; it does just the opposite—it *creates* financial insecurity! We can just as easily program ourselves to be financially insolvent, get by, or get ahead. Having enough or having a little extra means a lot to most people. But we were taught to tell ourselves the exact *opposite* of what we need to hear to make it work.

"I am good at earning what I need, and more! I'm good at saving money. Every month, without fail, I put

something aside. Each week, each month, and each year, I become financially secure." Give your mind the right direction, the right *challenge,* and it will work just as hard to make things work *for* you as it has worked to hold you back.

Your subconscious mind has not found it difficult to make things tight financially—it just did what you told it to do. If *you* don't make the change, neither will it. If you want to build a better financial base, have a talk with your subconscious. Tell it to do what you want it to do. The results may not come overnight, but they will come.

Example Seven:

Change the words **"I wish I had more time,"** to the words "*I make time and I take time to do what I need to do.*" Almost no one has *no* time to spare. Even the busiest people can find the time they need to do what they truly *choose* to do; the problem usually comes up when we forget that we have some choice in how we spend our time. If not having enough time is a problem, I would also add: "*I am responsible for choosing when, where, and how I spend my time. And I choose to spend my time in a way that creates the greatest benefits in my life.*"

Those few words of Self-Talk, spoken often enough, and at every opportunity, put *you* back in control. The result may be that you read a book on managing your time and put the ideas you get into practice. You may find yourself taking on fewer commitments, saying "no" more often, rearranging your schedule, or wasting less time and spending more time doing the things you'd like to get done.

That's how Self-Talk works. It gives your subconscious mind a specific set of directions and tells it to go to work on the problem. If you feed it the right directions, it will come up with the right solutions.

Those are just a few examples of how we can turn our words around—in specific Self-Talk phrases—anytime we'd like to. Given some thought, most of us could come up with dozens of examples of our own. Each of them can be reworded in the same way.

I find that it helps to write the old words down on paper. It makes it easier to see why it hasn't worked when you read it back to yourself. If you have a problem area, or an area of opportunity you would like to work on, try writing it out. Use the old words— state what is wrong and what you would like to do. Then take each thought, each sentence, and look at it. What have you said to yourself about it in the past? If the words you have been giving yourself were words of question, doubt, or negative acceptance, turn them around, one by one, and change them.

When you reword old self-talk (the negative kind) into new Self-Talk, it is important that you word it in the right way. The following checklist will help you check yourself on some of the "do's" and "don'ts" of writing Self-Talk:

THE SELF-TALK CHECK LIST

1. *IS YOUR SELF-TALK STATED IN THE PRESENT TENSE?*

Always state your Self-Talk in the present tense ("I

am . . ." "It is . . ." etc.). This is true of every form of Self-Talk other than "Situational Self-Talk" which was discussed in Chapter Twenty. In all other forms of Self-Talk the image you are creating for your subconscious mind should be a completed picture of you already having accomplished the objective.

2. *IS IT SPECIFIC?*

Be specific. State the details. Cover every possible facet of the problem or goal. Vague directions lead to vague results. The more specific you are, the more specific the directions you will be giving yourself.

3. *DOES IT GET THE JOB DONE WITHOUT CREATING ANY UNWANTED SIDE EFFECTS?*

Always add Self-Talk which directs you to achieve your objectives in a healthy and beneficial way. I recall the story of a woman who told herself she would do *anything* necessary to lose thirty-five pounds. It worked. She became ill, with an apparently unrelated illness, went into the hospital, and lost the weight.

It is fine to tell yourself that "nothing" will stop you from reaching your goal, whatever it is, but it is a good idea to add a few words of additional programming which tells your subconscious that you will reach that goal in a safe and worthwhile way.

Your subconscious mind is an incredibly powerful, goal-achieving mechanism. Programmed strongly enough, it will do *anything* necessary to help you achieve your goals. Unless you tell it what to do, it doesn't know the difference between right and wrong.

Make sure the words you give yourself tell your sub-conscious mind to get the job done in a way that is healthy and beneficial for all concerned.

4. *IS IT EASY TO USE?*

Good Self-Talk is simple Self-Talk. It should be easy to recall and use any time you need it. If it isn't, you won't use it. Use simple words which paint clear pictures.

5. *IS IT PRACTICAL?*

This doesn't mean that you can't use Self-Talk to help you dream dreams and turn them into reality. But the visions you create for yourself should be planted in good solid ground. If you program yourself to achieve the impossible, you will create frustration and failure. Stretch your limits, reach for your highest expectations, and tell yourself that you can achieve the best.

You can even go beyond what you once thought you could attain—and you should! But don't start demanding miracles of yourself until you have learned how to fix some of the everyday problems and reach some readily attainable goals. If you get really good, there will be time enough for miracles later.

6. *IS IT PERSONAL AND IS IT HONEST?*

When you are talking to yourself—talk to your*self*, and don't beat around the bush. One of the prime reasons for changing old self-talk into new is to give yourself a better way to deal with the facts—where you've been and where you're going, who you *thought* you were and who you really would like to be.

The only way to stop yourself from reliving the roadblocks that have stopped you in the past is to be honest about them. See them for what they are—or were. Take stock of yourself as you are now and set your sights on how you would like to become.

7. DOES YOUR SELF-TALK ASK ENOUGH OF YOU?

Just as it is important for each of us to keep our feet on the ground, it is important to expect from ourselves the best that we have to offer. Your Self-Talk should motivate you to go for the challenge, overcome the odds, and emerge the victor.

Since the subconscious mind does not know the difference between victory and defeat—it just acts on the impulses we give it—we might as well become winners in life instead of accepting anything less. Make sure your own Self-Talk demands the best of you.

Whether our goals are as simple as dealing with a daily problem or as exalted as making an important change in the direction of our lives, there is no reason to accept anything less than the greatest potential that each of us has within us. Your own individual Self-Talk should be a reflection of the greatest potential that you already hold within you. Never *ever* sell yourself short. Make sure your Self-Talk reaches in, grabs hold, and pulls the best out of you.

When you write or use Self-Talk in any form, keep this checklist in mind. If your own Self-Talk follows those guidelines, instead of ever having to worry about programming yourself in the wrong way, you can rest assured that you will be giving yourself the right directions—and you will be setting yourself up for getting the right results.

If you are not prone to sitting down and writing things out, you can achieve positive results just by becoming conscious of your own past self-talk and changing it accordingly. But deciding which new Self-Talk directions to use will be easier if you write them out. And, if you write out a few simple Self-Talk scripts which are written just for you, it will also make it easier for you to attempt, and succeed at, recording your self-suggestions on tape.

MAKING YOUR OWN SELF-TALK TAPES

If you would like to dive in and energetically pursue a personal Self-Talk program to tackle a goal or make some changes, listening to Self-Talk tapes can give you a positive boost in the right direction. Repeated playings of Self-Talk cassettes turn external Self-Talk (the words on the tape) into internal motivation—the important kind of self-motivation that stays with you.

Listening to Self-Talk tapes is not essential to using Self-Talk, but it makes the process of changing your old programming habits easier and faster. By now you are probably already using some of the Self-Talk techniques we have discussed. Even if you have just started being more aware of what you are saying and how you say it—you're headed in the right direction!

If you keep doing that, you will become a successful

Self-Talker with or without listening to Self-Talk tapes. But you may want to try recording a cassette or two to get the feel of it. If you have ever listened to a commercially produced Self-Talk cassette you already know what an experience that can be and what it can do for you.

When I first wrote and recorded Self-Talk tapes for myself, I was as hesitant about actually doing it as anyone who is attempting a home, do-it-yourself recording for the first time. Few of us are recording engineers or professional speakers; making something even as simple as a voice recording on a cassette can be a little intimidating. It needn't be. And if you would like to try it for yourself, there are a few suggestions which will help.

THE OUTSIDE VOICE OF ENCOURAGEMENT AND AUTHORITY

Don't worry about how you may feel your own voice sounds on a tape recording—Self-Talk cassettes work better when the voice on the tape is someone's other than your own. We tend to believe someone *else* telling us good things about ourselves before we believe ourselves. We grew up listening to outside voices of authority; we were conditioned to accept what someone else told us more than we were conditioned to accept our own opinions about ourselves. That is one of the things that becoming a self-directed Self-Talker changes. But for now, an outside voice works better.

When you record your new Self-Talk, enlist the aid

of a trusted friend or associate—someone whose opinions you already value. Ask that friend to read your Self-Talk script on the tape. After even a short time of listening to a Self-Talk cassette, the voice you are hearing on the tape will become an "inner voice" and you will begin to hear *yourself* talking to you, *internally,* instead of paying attention to the actual recorded voice you are listening to.

Keep your Self-Talk tapes short—about eighteen to twenty-two minutes. Self-Talk tapes should be designed to be used frequently, not occasionally in one long sitting.

PRESENT TENSE, POSITIVE FORM

For the actual script you use to create your tape, follow the earlier suggestions about writing a reworded Self-Talk script. Write out fifteen to eighteen self-suggestions, all worded in the form of Level III or Level IV Self-Talk. Most of them should use the Level IV wording which was discussed in Chapter Nine and earlier in this chapter—positive Self-Talk statements which show you a picture of yourself having already accomplished the goal. ("I weigh 147 slim, trim, attractive pounds," or "I am always on time," etc.)

On the tape, repeat each of the suggestions three times, with a short pause in between each of them. Then go on to the next self-suggestion, again repeating it three times, until you have completed your list of Self-Talk phrases.

End the tape by recording each of the phrases one additional time each, but this time change "I" to

"*You.*" "*I* am a good listener; *I* enjoy hearing what others have to say," becomes "*You* are a good listener; *you* enjoy hearing what other people have to say." The reason for doing this is that it recognizes our need to have external validation—someone else telling us we are doing a good job.

MUSIC AND THE SUBCONSCIOUS MIND

In the tapes which I subsequently recorded (in a studio), appropriate music was added to the last "You" portion of each tape. There is a technical "programming" reason for doing this, having to do with how the brain responds to *emotional* input. The music adds an element which balances the logical, structured Self-Talk with input which creates feelings and stimulates the imagination. Have you ever noticed that listening to a certain kind of music can sometimes instantly change your mood?

Although adding the right music adds to the effectiveness of your recorded Self-Talk, you can achieve the same results by listening to your Self-Talk cassettes while you are playing music on a separate cassette player or from a record.

There has been a great deal of research done on the effects of certain kinds of music on learning. Music which is performed at a specific number of beats per minute seems to affect the way the brain receives and stores information. If your interest is in extracting the most from your Self-Talk that you can possibly get, and you would like to learn more about the effects of recording and listening to specific kinds of music with your Self-Talk, you may want to start by reading the book *Super-Learning* by Sheila Ostrander and Lynn Schroeder (1979, Dell Publishing).

The principle benefit, however, of listening to Self-Talk on cassettes is that this form of learning and practicing Self-Talk lets you work at it without having to *work* at it—you can listen to a cassette tape while you are busy doing something else. Listening to Self-Talk on cassettes is a practical and convenient way to have that internal "coach" standing by whenever you need it, ready to tell you the best about yourself. Cassettes are not essential to your growth as a positive, productive Self-Talker, but I would encourage you to try them. They will encourage you in your efforts, remind you of your goals, give you support when you need it most, and add an important lift in your attitude throughout the day.

CHAPTER TWENTY-THREE

To Change or Not to Change

AT THIS MOMENT, or at some time in the future, you may make the decision to make a change. Let me give you a few words of encouragement. It is likely that you already know what you would like to do. If that is the case, if your innermost mind tells you that it is time, then it is time.

When Shakespeare wrote the words "To be or not to be . . ." he may not have known that he touched the essence of *self*. To *be* or not to *be*, that *is* the question. To become or not to become; to achieve or not to achieve; to *do* or not to do—the answer to that question is the answer which will determine the future—and the success—of each of us.

It's a good idea to take stock of our progress. It is healthy to ask ourselves how well we are doing. We have the right and the need to gauge, judge, and assess our own forward motion. *Are we getting anywhere or aren't we? Are we getting by or are we doing the best that we can? Are we doing what we want to do or would we like to do something else, something better? Do we have every part of ourselves in line and in tune* with our finest expectations, or would we like to make a change or two?

Most of us have changes we would like to make in our lives. There are times when we want to make a small change, something that will help us do something differently, or deal with something in a better way than we dealt with it in the past. There are other times when we would like to make a sweeping change—out with the old and in with the new!

If making life "work" is as simple as making a few changes, why don't you do it?

WOULD YOU LIKE TO MAKE A CHANGE?

I have known people who wanted nothing more than to fix a problem at home or at work, or wanted to change some small thing about themselves or in their lives that would help them grow or make life a little easier. I have also known people who were fed up with everything. They wanted to change their lives in a major way—different job, new husband or wife, sell out and move to another state—they wanted to do whatever it would take to change their lives and change their futures. I have known people who tried to change their lives by changing their homes, cars, or careers.

But for the most of them the *change* wasn't a real change; it didn't work! They took their old selves with them. Changes of heart are as fragile and as temporary as changes of costumes in a play. We can change friends, spouses, jobs, or locations, and we will still take the same inner selves along with us—the same internal identities which made us unhappy, helped us, or got us into trouble in the first place. If we take the old images of ourselves with us wherever we go and into whatever we do, how could we expect to do better the next time we try?

If we want to make any important change in our beliefs, attitudes, emotions, behavior, actions, or results, we should, at the outset, decide who is in command—and who or what is in control of the changes that take place.

How would you identify the changes that are happening in your life? Are they the result of accident, destiny, circumstance, or personal decision?

Change occurs either as a result of something outside of you that happens *to you*, or as a result of something within yourself which causes the change to take place.

CHANGE CREATED BY EXTERNAL INFLUENCES

With this kind of change there is no major psychological impact which alerts us to the fact that the change is happening. There is nothing traumatic about this kind of change—in fact there is nothing noticeable about it at all. This change happens normally and casually: it is the result of the relentless, unseen waves of external influence, day after day, hour by hour, shaping and reshaping the shorelines of our thinking.

The kind of change which happens *to* us is the result of those minor attitude changes which come to us by way of expectations, minor events, company policies, personal relationships, relatives, family needs, parental authority, religious credos, peer pressures, advertising of all kinds, economic trends, daily exposure to television, radio, magazines and newspapers, social requirements, political positions, whimsical notions, close friends, and off-hand comments.

It is strange that these influences should shape most of our lives for us; and yet they do. They are not all bad or contrary of course—some of them are necessary and worthwhile. Some of these influences—a few of them—are the best kind we can ever hope to find. But taken as a group, these everyday influences in our lives are seldom the notes on which great symphonies are played. More often they are dirges, plainly-written tunes, written in the key of average, with a slowly meandering discordant melody, leading to something less than the rising crescendo of great finales we had hoped for, never once demanding or creating the lasting and beautiful orchestration of a life well-lived.

The conditioning of daily living somehow convinces us that mankind's greatest need, *social survival,* is also each person's greatest achievement!

The result is that we slowly, unknowingly, change— not to achieve—but to *survive,* in a way that offers us the acceptance of others. We get by. We do what we must. We do as well as we can, get along with others as well as possible, play our roles, do our jobs, put a little away for the future, and hope for the best. *The dreams we dreamed as children, we learn no longer to believe.*

That is the tune we are taught to play. Instead of

believing, *knowing,* that each of us is an entire orchestra, we are led to believe we are only the flute. We listen to the idle gossip of a friend, follow the lead of so-called leaders, fit our lives into a mold that was not of our making, tuck our dreams in our pockets, and hope for better things to come.

And so we are changed by the lives we live. For most of us it is seldom the calamitous change of catastrophic events. It is the slow, sure change of environment—the change forced upon us by the world around us. What we become a part *of* becomes a part of *us.* What we perceive and what we accept is an important part of what we too will become.

THE ALTERNATIVE CHANGE
CREATED BY PERSONAL CHOICE

The one kind of change in our lives which is left up to the individual—to each of us—is the change which is created by personal *choice*.

Have you ever thought about the fact that what you do, how you live, what you become, is almost entirely up to you? Of course there are outside circumstances to deal with, but how you deal with them is still, and finally, up to no one else but you. *What you decide to do next will determine what you do next*.

Make the decision to do what you choose and your next step will be your own. Sit back and let the outside world take the lead and it will. Decide to determine your own next step—and thereby your future—and you can. Make the decision to make each breath you breathe your own. Stick by it, and each breath, step, motion, and achievement will be of your own making and of your own choice.

The research of neuroscience has proved that what you determine for yourself, what you conceive and give your energies to, will create or call upon a life force which will turn the dreams you dream into touchable reality. But we have only recently learned the process that makes it work: *learn how to think what you think and you will begin to determine and redirect most of your future for yourself.* If you learn *how* to think *what* you think, you will put yourself back in control.

Just as it is the thoughts, ideas, demands, and influences of others which have guided, controlled, and directed most of our lives in the past, it is the personal control of our own minds which now gives us the chance to change our futures—for ourselves.

You can do so much. You can, if you choose, break through the wall that stands between you and anything you would like to change or achieve. Give yourself the will to do it. Give yourself the belief, the attitude, the emotion, and the action that will get you where you want to be.

THE FINAL DIFFERENCE

We began this journey through the workings of the mind and through the maze of possible solutions with my own personal search for an answer that not only would work, but would keep on working. Temporary success is fine, but something that turns temporary success into a permanent way of life makes a lot more sense. Living each day in a more successful way is what each of us, somewhere within us, would like to achieve.

There are no magic formulas—of that I am sure. There are no quick solutions or overnight fixes. We are overcome with those. Name the problem or the goal and we can find the book or the advice which tells us how to fix it, or create it—for a time.

In many ways, we have come so far. We have achieved almost unimagined heights in our technology, in our material wealth. At our least, we have more conveniences, more tools, more appliances of life, than the wealthiest of kings and queens had in their lives only a few decades ago. Through our medicine and our science, we have extended the potential for living more years on earth than was ever thought possible even a few generations in the past. We have conquered the shallow envelope of space which surrounds us. We have learned to manage our businesses, some of our environment, and a small part of our destinies.

But we have not yet learned to manage the one part of our lives which is the heart and substance of everything we will ever do. We have not yet learned to manage our own minds.

THE SOLUTION

Learning to manage, control, and direct the resources of your mind is the greatest challenge you will ever face.

WHAT TO SAY WHEN YOU TALK TO YOUR SELF

The key to all management, the management of others, the management of your resources, and the management of your future, is Self-Management.

Self-Management is the difference between living a life of fulfillment and purpose, and living out our years frustrated and incomplete, contained by the short-sighted limitations of our own disbelief. Self-Management is the final conquest. And its solution is within our reach.

Until recently we haven't even known the name of our greatest adversary—that wall which has confined us to the smallest part of what we could have been. The adversary has been *us*. It is the thoughts which we have thought. It is our own thinking which has created the limited self-portraits of who we believed ourselves to be.

Our technology has taught us something. Our emerging understanding of our own human brain has pointed us in the right direction. We have learned that what we do, and what we do with *us,* is not an accidental happening. We have learned that *who* we are and *what* we are is the result of more than a chance combination of genetic inclinations. We have learned that what happens next—for each of us—is more up to us than we might have *thought:* it is up to what we *think.*

Talk to yourself! Learn the words—the *right* words—and use them. Make your Self-Talk an everyday, unconscious, self-directing habit. Talk to yourself in a way that is *kind, loving, caring, strong, demanding,* and *determined.* Talk to yourself in the right way, every day.

When you do, you will give yourself the greatest gift you will ever give.

WHAT TO SAY WHEN YOU TALK TO YOUR SELF

Remember,

You are everything that is,
Your thoughts, your life, your dreams come true.
You are everything you choose to be.
You are as unlimited as the endless universe.

For more information, write:

"Self-Talk"
Dept. S-1, P.O. Box 5165
Scottsdale, AZ, 85261